"*Enhancing Pleasure for Gay Men* provides a sure-to-be-indispensable guide with a pleasure-centered ethos that is steeped in intersectional approaches and social justice methods. It not only raises awareness of specific issues of vital concerns to gay male clients, but also provides ethical and effective resources and tools to enhance clinical practice and promote greater empathic attunement."

Lucie Fielding, *PhD, author of* Trans Sex: Clinical Approaches to Trans Sexualities and Erotic Embodiments

"In a nonjudgmental, respectful and non-pathologizing way, Martinez explains the unique role sex has played for gay men. Not only does he offer numerous strategies for resolving specific sexual issues, he postulates that sex can heal larger 'developmental, attachment and systems' issues for gay men. Thus, this clinical guide is thoroughly sex positive!"

Gil Tunnell, *PhD, co-author of* Couple Therapy with Gay Men

"In *Enhancing Pleasure for Gay Men*, Israel has provided a comprehensive, candid, clinically-sound, and practical framework that informs and invites clinicians to more effectively help gay male clients work on their complicated and misunderstood relationship to pleasure so they can feel free to have more pleasurable sex."

Buck Dodson, *LCSW, creator and host of Gay Men's Life Lab*

Enhancing Pleasure for Gay Men

This book aims to help therapists understand the challenges gay men face in their sex lives, providing professionals and gay men with evidence-based interventions and clinical tools to help them heal and live overall healthier lives.

Gay men have unique and debilitating issues that can get in the way of them having pleasurable sex. Instead of sex being a space to learn about themselves, heal, release, and receive joy, for many sex is fraught with shame, anxiety, self-hate, and feeling isolated. Written for both professionals and the clients they treat, this book aims to heal sex-related wounds through sex and, in turn, improve every aspect of gay men's mental health. The book begins by exploring what is special about gay men and sex before looking at assessing and presenting medical and psychological issues impacting sexual functioning, such as childhood trauma, attachment styles, body issues, anxiety, depression, long-term relationships and parenting, and hookup apps. It then moves onto clinical interventions to address these issues, with intake questionnaires and information on how to adapt sensate focus exercises, neuroscience, narrative, CBT, and somatic modalities to provide sex therapy interventions specific to gay men.

With special focus on marginalized communities within the LGBTQIA+ community, such as trans men, BIPOC, aging, disabled, and chronically ill voices, this book is essential reading for sex therapists and mental health professionals working with gay men, as well as gay men themselves looking to live authentically and happily in their sexual lives.

Israel Martinez (he/him) has his doctorate in clinical sexology and is a psychotherapist, lecturer, and supervisor. He has been working with gay men clinically for over 15 years and is the author of *Helping Gay Men Find Love*.

Enhancing Pleasure for Gay Men

A Clinical Guide for Healing and Acceptance Through Better Sex

Israel Martinez

Routledge
Taylor & Francis Group

NEW YORK AND LONDON

Designed cover image: Timsulov © Getty Images

First published 2025
by Routledge
605 Third Avenue, New York, NY 10158

and by Routledge
4 Park Square, Milton Park, Abingdon, Oxon, OX14 4RN

Routledge is an imprint of the Taylor & Francis Group, an informa business

© 2025 Israel Martinez

The right of Israel Martinez to be identified as author of this work has been asserted in accordance with sections 77 and 78 of the Copyright, Designs and Patents Act 1988.

ISBN: 978-1-032-47871-5 (hbk)
ISBN: 978-1-032-47870-8 (pbk)
ISBN: 978-1-003-38632-2 (ebk)

DOI: 10.4324/9781003386322

Typeset in Times New Roman
by SPi Technologies India Pvt Ltd (Straive)

Access the Support Material:
www.routledge.com/9781032478708

This book is dedicated to two authors who were instrumental in the healing that allowed me to thrive, Bruce Bawer and Alan Downs.

Contents

Introduction

Gay men are not safe. To downplay the unique mental health challenges with which gay men have to contend would greatly harm our community. This is a group which, up until the 1970s, was classified as deviant by the Diagnostic and Statistical Manual of Mental Disorders (DSM), could not legally marry another man in this country on a national level until 2015 (and still have to contend with most people referring to it as "gay marriage" instead of just "marriage"), and could not legally have sex in every state of the United States until 2003. And this is a community that has suffered through an epidemic that unmercifully killed a third of a million people over a period of just 15 years (Odets, 2019). Most of those who died of AIDS were gay men, with the disease being the leading cause of death for young adult men in San Francisco, Los Angeles, and New York City during this period (Center for Disease Control, 1991). And while gay men have been granted rights and protections in the last couple of decades, the most recent appointees to the Supreme Court of the United States are socially illiberal and have moved the Court to a conservative majority. Many states, institutions, and businesses are looking to take this opportunity to rescind rights that were granted to LGBTQ+ individuals on a national level, including gay men. At the time of this writing, almost 40 states in this country have at least one anti-LGBTQ+ bill up for consideration (Freedom for All Americans, n.d.). States have begun signing into law bills that ban public school teachers from holding classroom instruction on anything related to sexual orientation or gender identity, are banning life-saving gender-affirming care, and are successfully stopping LGBTQ+ people from marching in parades. These are scary times for gay men, a community that has a long history of being marginalized and stigmatized and, from childhood, having to hide their true selves in order to survive.

Please do not underestimate the needs of your gay clients. They have a plethora of unique stressors that need to be specifically addressed in order

DOI: 10.4324/9781003386322-1

to truly heal and they must attain as many resources and skills as possible to improve their mental health and allow them to thrive. There are already books available to help clinicians who want to learn how to work with gay men. What I offer here is a whole new platform that will teach you how to enhance sexual pleasure for your gay male clients, allowing them to experience overall better health. We will work together to focus on removing obstacles, providing resources, and teaching skills that lead to better sex so that your gay male clients heal and see themselves in a more realistic way.

You might be thinking to yourself, "Wait. Aren't gay men known to have lots of sex?" And you would be correct. They are "known" for this. It is an assumption that gay men are having tons of sex. While there are some gay men who are having a lot of sex, that does not mean they are necessarily deriving pleasure from this sex or that it is something that is contributing to their well-being. There are also a lot of gay men who stay away from sex because they feel unworthy, shame related to having sex with other men, and insecurity about their bodies not fitting a very specific aesthetic of what is considered desirable among gay men. Some gay men also deal with issues around erection, pain while bottoming (anodyspareunia), and libido concerns. These issues do not stay relegated to affecting just sexual encounters. They bleed into all areas of one's life and therefore contribute to a poorer quality of mental health and overall life satisfaction.

I have seen how healing a person's sexual issues improves their whole life because sex-related wounds tend to touch so many non-sexual parts of one's life. I have also experienced clients' innate drive to free themselves from "psychological inhibitions and suffering" (Bader, 2002, p. 8) through sexual fantasy and arousal. For those who are sexual beings, sex, happiness, health, and life satisfaction are all intertwined. This book will show you how you can play your part in finally allowing gay men to have the sex they deserve and, through this, liberate them from the mental health and substance issues they face in greater percentages than their straight peers. We will begin this journey by discussing the additional challenges for gay men around mental health, substance abuse, and sex. Once that is established, the book will educate you on how to ethically and effectively address each of those challenges using various clinical methods. The interventions presented will come from peer-reviewed journal articles, evidence and research-based books, and my experiences as a clinician.

Intersectionality

Throughout this book you will notice an emphasis on intersectionality. Kimberlé Crenshaw first introduced the concept of intersectionality, which speaks to how, as individuals, we have many parts to our identities that can lead to discrimination and to privilege. Levantino (2022) states the following:

> An intersectional examination of systems of power and privilege reveals that those closest to dominant identities are afforded more comfort, privilege, and power without expending additional work or effort. Those with identity attributes further from individuals in power receive increased levels of discrimination, prejudice, and threat to physical and mental harm, and, as a result, fewer opportunities for advancement.
>
> (p. 328)

Gay men are discriminated against, and gay men who are BIPOC (Black, Indigenous, and/or a Person of Color), disabled, chronically ill, not cisgender, fat, and/or older face even more intense discrimination; "For example, a financially affluent, young, straight acting, white, abled, cisgender gay-identifying male is afforded more opportunities (and less likely to experience discrimination) than a transgender, differently abled woman of color" (Levantino, 2022, p. 328). It is no secret that increased likelihood of discrimination leads to increased likelihood of mental health issues. In each chapter I will try to address these issues around intersectionality for gay men to the best of my ability, using: 1) the scant amount of research available that has studied gay men who are a part of these further marginalized communities and 2) experiences from my own clinical practice.

Gay Men Not Represented in this Book

An intersectionality for gay men that I would like to make you aware of but will not be discussing in this book is that of asexual and aromantic gay men. While a small portion of this group does engage in sex, I do not have experience healing these men through sex and therefore do not feel comfortable prescribing specific ways to do so.

Another intersectionality that I do not have experience healing through sex are gay men with an intellectual and/or developmental disability. Despite popular opinion, this group is sexual. Onstot (2019) warns us that false beliefs that this community is unable to understand and practice sex education and that sex can only be harmful for them leads to paternalistic practices have kept this community from being able to have sex. Please do not take my lack of current experience with gay men with an intellectual and/or developmental disability as an indication that I believe they are not, or should not, be having sex.

I will also not be writing about bisexual or pansexual men in this book. While, like gay men, they have an attraction to men, also having an attraction to genders outside of men gives this community a completely different identity than gay men. Please do not take my distinguishing between gay men and bisexual or pansexual men as my belief that these men are not as marginalized as gay men. Actually, I am quite aware that, unlike most gay men, their full identity often goes unacknowledged, because others label them based on the gender appearance of the person(s) they are in a relationship with at the time. And their lack of being wholly acknowledged is true even within the queer community, as many in the queer community have the false belief that bisexuality or pansexuality is not a valid sexual orientation, but instead a way to deny or avoid coming to terms with being gay or lesbian. Taylor, Power, Smith, and Rathbone (2019) found that feelings of invisibility were an important factor related to poor mental health for the bisexual community. And, in general, mental health issues are more severe for those who are bisexual or pansexual, even when compared to their lesbian and gay counterparts (Taylor, Power, Smith, & Rathbone, 2019). One reason behind this is they have to face not only homophobia and heterosexism, but also biphobia and monosexism (the belief that exclusive heterosexuality and/or homosexuality is superior).

Enthusiastic Consent

We cannot talk about sex without discussing consent. As clinicians, we must understand the vital importance of consent when it comes to any sex-related activities. Consent must be an enthusiastic yes to something. Silence as a response to something is in no way equal to consent and anyone is able, at any point, to change their mind about that with which they wish to consent. Being on substances and in certain states of mind can easily get in the way of consent being properly given and should never be used as an excuse for not getting an enthusiastic yes for consent. Even sex play where the premise is that there is no consent, needs actual consent and detailed agreements about what will happen during and after play in order to allow that type of scenario to be able to be played out. Please ensure your clients understand what consent is, for their own sake and for the sake of their partners.

Labels

My intent with the labels and pronouns I use in this book is to be as realistic as possible about the many types of beings that exist in our world. When I use the terms gay men, gay males, or gay boys I am referring to anyone who identifies as such and I do not assume that they all have the same anatomy. In order to properly represent the studies referenced in this book, I will use the labeling provided by the authors of those articles or books, even if I do not agree with their choice of terminology.

Case Studies

The case studies I present here are a conglomerate of various clients I have seen and not purely representative of any one client. I have done my best to honor the confidentiality of all persons depicted in these case studies.

Lenape Land

I want to show my gratitude to and acknowledge the Lenape tribe, whose ancestral homeland I am writing this book from and on whom I have built my clinical practice.

What to Expect

This book will help you understand why using sex as a tool to heal gay men is especially powerful. You will receive a history lesson on what role sex has played in the lives and identities of gay men, showing how their heterosexual counterparts did not, for the most part, have sex play such a major role in defining them as a community and individuals. Examples to illustrate this will include how the very label (and therefore identity) of "gay" is often defined by society in terms of whom one has sex with. Gay boys feel they have had their first gay experience only when first being sexual with another male, and the AIDS crisis starkly linked the death or survival of gay individuals to how they chose to have sex. I will also illustrate the trauma experienced by gay men living through the AIDS crisis and help you better understand the prevalence among gay men of combining illegal drugs and sex.

I will also challenge the preconceived notions you may have around gay men and sex and help you assess what biases (we all have some) you are bringing into session that may be causing clients further harm. You will gain a more robust and evidence-based understanding of the concept of "sex addiction" and why gay men often will incorrectly receive and get pathologized by this label. Other important misconceptions I will correct include that gay men are not wired for monogamy, that there is a need for monogamy in order to be in a healthy relationship, and that they only have sex in one particular way (usually including anal penetration).

Since medical issues always need to be considered when assessing a sexual issue with anyone. This book will advise on: 1) how to look for possible biological or physiological issues that may be getting in the way of sexual functioning for gay men, 2) what medications to be aware of, and 3) the world of medical professions that can be harmful to gay men.

You will then gain insight into the childhood development story of most gay men, the most common attachment style that gay men develop, and how consistently gay men are marginalized and stigmatized (from blatant homophobia to microaggressions) by systems, including family, friends, community, and government policies.

While we live in a world that bombards us with impossible images and messaging about what our bodies "should" look like, gay men have their own set of unrealistic standards. You will learn how body issues for gay men are caused by: 1) an increased need for external validation, 2) living within a community that is especially age-obsessed and has a very narrow view of what is sexy, and 3) extra susceptibility to toxic masculinity (when compared to their heterosexual counterparts).

I will explain how the minority status of gay men contributes to increased anxiety and how this anxiety gets in the way of sex. You will see how the shame of growing up as a gay boy, sex starting out as secretive and "dirty" and continuing that way, heteronormativity, homophobia, internalized heterosexism, increased usage of alcohol and drugs to cope, religion, and a higher likelihood of being isolated can lead to depressive symptoms.

You will also see what sexual issues may transpire in gay male relationships. Though gay male relationships have been shown to be just as healthy as or healthier than heterosexual relationships, there are unique obstacles gay male relationships experience. I will explain the difficulty of looking to create an intimate relationship with a male when as a child survival meant hiding yourself and not being vulnerable to other males. I will also show how increased mental health issues for gay men lead to increased chances of mental health issues being present in a relationship between two men, getting in the way of healthy sex. You will see how libido discordance gets stigmatized and leads to avoidance of sex because of the societal belief that "proper" men are supposed to always want sex. I will address how cross-generational relationships (which have a higher prevalence of occurring within gay relationships than heterosexual ones), the degree to which a partner is out, and HIV discordance increase the likelihood of sexual discrepancy issues. And, since many gay men are in some type of non-monogamous relationship, I will explain the added hurdles of dealing with ethical non-monogamous relationships.

When exploring gay men and their relationship to sex, one must be familiar with the traps and gifts offered by hookup apps. I will shed light on how the anonymity present in hookup apps lends to toxic behavior and mistreatment of others on these apps. I will also speak to the addictive nature that gets intensified by relying on hookup apps for validation and make clear the rampant and explicit shaming that happens over race, body type, disposition (mostly around a narrow-minded binary concept of being masculine or feminine), age, and penis size. And I will shed light on the ease of finding illegal drugs on these apps that get used during sex.

To transition us into treatment, I will provide a suggested sex therapy intake conversation tailored to gay men, with the hopes of enhancing your ability to effectively and ethically collect vital information for assessment. I will also explain how the language we use on such questionnaires can be further stigmatizing – terms like "dysfunction", "premature", "early", "delayed", "low", and "high" – and provide readers with more representative language related to sexual issues.

The main focus of this book will be: interventions. I will provide guidance on how to get your clients to the medical professionals who are more likely to help them. I will also explain how to work with clients to prepare them for that first doctor's visit. You will also learn how to teach clients: 1) the squeeze and stop-and-start techniques, 2) about medications and surgeries that may interfere with sex, 3) how to safely use medications that help with erection, 4) how to work to try to resolve ejaculation issues and anodyspareunia (pain during receptive anal sex), and 5) which sex toys and lube are safe and make the most sense for their bodies and bottoming.

You will learn how to use techniques from Narrative Therapy to help clients work through issues that have come out of their childhood development and Relational Therapy to change attachment style. And I will provide ways for you to directly advocate for changes to systems that are oppressing gay men.

I will share how to address body issues for gay men, including normalizing their need for external validation, working on ways to create internal validation and get healthy external validation from friends and family, teaching techniques to increase self-compassion and radical self-love, and introducing the option of body neutrality. I will also address how transgender and non-binary individuals tend to differ when it comes to body image issues.

How to use Cognitive Behavior Therapy (CBT), the Dual Control Model, sexual menus, and pain management to treat issues specific to gay men will be shown. You will also be provided interventions for sexual compulsion and managing sexually transmitted infections. I will demonstrate how to use the PLISSIT Model and sensate focus to deal with the trauma of sexual abuse. In addition, Dialectal Behavior Therapy (DBT) techniques will be used as the main therapeutic intervention for clients to address the issues specific to gay men that lead to depression. We will also address ways to reduce shame and the harm caused by religious institutions, as well as how to how treat substance issues specific to gay men.

Aspects from the Developmental Model of Couples Therapy will serve as a guide for clients looking to improve communication. And you will learn how to intervene on issues related to arousal and vulnerability, work with consensually non-monogamous relationships, and help sex happen as a parent.

You will also learn how to work with your clients to safely and with intentionality make use of hookup apps.

I will provide general solutions to increase sexual health and pleasure for gay men, including detail on which body parts tend to be most primed to receive pleasure, specific tips for gay men who are part of aging, transgender, non-binary, disabled and/or chronic ill communities, and the fundamentals of kink/bondage, discipline/domination, sadism/submission, and masochism (BDSM).

A detailed listing of resources that relate to gay men and sex and a glossary of terms are also provided.

References

Bader, M.J. (2002). *Arousal: The secret logic of sexual fantasies*. New York, NY: St. Martin's Press.

Center for Disease Control (January 25, 1991). Retrieved, February 12, 2023 from https://www.cdc.gov/mmwr/preview/mmwrhtml/00001880.htm

Freedom For All Americans (n.d.). Retrieved, November 22, 2021 from https://freedomforallamericans.org/legislative-tracker/anti-transgender-legislation/

Levantino, P.D. (2022). "I didn't know I had a right to exist": Queer elders and family therapy. In R. Harvey, M.J. Murphy, J.J. Bigner, & J.L. Wetchler (Eds.), *Handbook of LGBTQ-Affirmative couple and family therapy*. New York, NY: Routledge.

Odets, W. (2019). *Out of the shadows: Reimagining gay men's lives*. New York, NY: Picador.

Onstot, A. (2019). Capacity to consent: Policies and practices that limit sexual consent for people with intellectual/developmental disabilities. *Sexuality and Disability 37*, 633–644.

Taylor, J., Power, J., Smith, E., & Rathbone, M. (2019). Bisexual mental health. *Australian Journal of General Practice, 48*(3), 138–144.

Chapter 1

The Unique Role Sex Has Played for Gay Men

Sex in the Dark

Darkness. A man in a rarely used public restroom looking for a glory hole. Darkness. A man walking at night through a section of park known for cruising. Darkness. A kid with a flashlight under his sheets looking at a department store catalog, focusing on the buff guys in underwear. Darkness. A man in a back dark room of a bar, unable to see the face of others and looking for anonymous sex. All this darkness can add to the excitement of sex, and it can also allow shame to flourish. Most gay men have grown up with attraction and sex being tied to secrecy and darkness. When I speak to darkness, I speak to the literal darkness just described and also a symbolic darkness of something "dirty" that they are engaging in, that if anyone found out about could mean their doom. Does the idea of doom seem exaggerated? Being found out as gay, even today, even in progressive and liberal states in the United States, could easily mean ostracization and, since human beings are social beings, would basically mean annihilation. Imagine something seen as so simple, expected, natural, and celebrated as a boy and girl liking each other being turned into a deviant feeling if it is a boy who likes another boy. How can you not feel wrong to your core when society (media, government, authority figures, friends, and family) is either overtly, through homophobia, or "subtly", through microaggressions and heteronormativity, consistently giving you this exact message? And what are the chances that any sex you have throughout your life, even in broad daylight, will not carry that stigma and cause shame?

Sex as an "Identity"

Gay men are labeled by most of the world as gay because they are men who do not fit with the "norm" of having sex with women. They are born into a society that sees and treats them as less than their heterosexual counterparts, because of who they are attracted to, and, ultimately, with whom they want

DOI: 10.4324/9781003386322-2

to have sex. Past sodomy laws (not invalidated on a federal level in the United States until 2003) outlawed sex that gay men have with one another as an attempt to suppress and erase gay men. And many religious sects will embrace you, even if you are gay, as long as you do not act on it, i.e., have sex with other men. Imagine if the very natural and beautiful act of consenting sex is what led to you being stigmatized and marginalized. This would obviously increase the likelihood that you would feel that the sex you were having was not natural or beautiful, and instead that it was something to be ashamed of.

And for most gay boys, their first "gay experience" was also wrapped up in sex. Sure, maybe they wore their mother's high heels around the house or twirled and sang musicals every chance they got as a kid. While those are behaviors common to the gay culture of boys, we would not likely deem either one of those as their first gay experience. Even if they we were lucky enough to date another boy publicly and take him to the prom, that is still not often known as a first gay experience. It is often decided that gay males do not truly have their first gay experience until they are sexually intimate with another male – reducing the gay male identity to just sex. And the sex they have is rarely the kind of sex that they get celebrated and patted on the back for, the way straight men do when they have sex for the first time. Instead, they likely do not tell another soul, for fear of being ostracized or physically harmed or killed because their sex is seen by society as dirty and wrong.

HIV

On a Monday, a young man attends the funeral of their 23-year-old friend. The next day he attends another funeral, this time for his 25-year-old neighbor. Thursday of that same week he attends one for a 22-year-old friend and the weekend brings with it three more funerals he will attend. During the AIDS crisis, for many, this was their reality. Their friends were dying in degrading and painful ways, often without biological family around to provide support and care. Instead, these men were relegated to hospitals where staff often did not want to touch them or offer comfort. They were being told that they deserved to die this way because of their "crime" – having sex with men. The devastating effects of the AIDS epidemic were felt not only by the multitudes who died such horrible deaths, but also by those who survived. They survived to see so many of their friends die and to live as part of a community that was decimated and robbed of great support and role models. All of this loss, society at large would have you believe, because of the type and frequency of sex that gay men have. Imagine your community living for decades with the reality that a plague wiped out so many and something as beautiful and natural as sex was made the center of the cause.

Imagine an epidemic so stigmatized around sex that many gay men stopped having sex altogether or switched to and stayed in monogamous relationships that were not actually a fit for their identity. This trauma does not disappear once HIV becomes treatable. It lingers and effects how gay men view sex today. Even when the treatment of HIV first started to become an option, sex for gay men still often revolved around HIV status. A lot of men that were HIV+ were shunned and considered (by themselves and others) as too dangerous for sex. The term "clean" came about to label those who were HIV- and who were considered safe and desirable sexual partners.

Even as treatment for HIV improved, and one could be HIV+ and undetectable (meaning that their HIV viral load was so low that it could not be measured, that therefore it was extremely unlikely that they could pass on the virus to another during sex), this did not wipe away the stigma of being HIV+ and allow all gay men, whether HIV+ or HIV-, to freely engage in sex and relationships. The concept of "clean" is very much alive today, being used to discriminate against having sex with those who are HIV+. Imagine having an infection that is stigmatized around sex, the messaging being that you are "dirty" for getting it and not fit to have sex or be in a relationship with others.

In 2012, an effective pre-exposure prophylaxis (PrEP) was introduced to reduce the risk of acquiring HIV. This was in the form of a pill taken once a day that, if taken properly, would leave you at only a very minimal risk of being able to contract HIV. One would hope that with PrEP being used and those who are HIV+ being able to be undetectable, we would make great leaps in equality in the gay male community when it came to sex and relationships. Unfortunately, that has not been the case. Those who decided to take PrEP were slut-shamed, being labeled reckless because many gay men saw them as increasing their frequency of sex and practicing less safer sex. Further, for many of those who lived through the AIDS epidemic, the idea of a pill that could keep gay men from getting HIV, allowing sex to occur in a style similar to before the AIDS epidemic, proved triggering. That even with the medical advances made to make HIV less likely to be transmitted and easier to live with, the gay community still uses it to divide itself, speaks to how ingrained the idea of shame and death became linked with gay sex throughout the AIDS epidemic.

Chem sex

A gay man is on his couch, feeling horny and lonely. He has access to a hookup app that can help him find someone with whom to have sex. However, he hesitates from enjoying something so beautiful and natural because shame is creeping in and telling him that his body is not hot enough and that no one would enjoy sex with him anyway, especially since he just turned 35 (a "dinosaur" in "gay years"). However, he knows that all of these insecurities will melt away if he takes crystal meth before having sex. And he knows that he can find a place, through the same hookup app, to access those drugs. Could it be any easier? He said that the last time would be his last time because when he comes off the drugs he is filled with shame and fear, wondering exactly what he did and what other drugs he took that weekend while under the influence of the meth. He is also reliably depressed while recovering, usually for a period of around three days. However, it is so easy to access the drugs that he thinks to himself, "I can't have sex right now without the drugs. This next time will definitely be my last time." He goes on the app looking for the profiles that clearly show they have meth available. "With Chemsex, there is an instant sense of connection, no rejection, no criticism of body image, sexual performance or age, everybody is welcome and everybody can enjoy their right of having sexual pleasure with no shame..." (Neves, 2021). Imagine it being so easy to access sex and the elixir that is going to wipe away all of the shame and struggles around sex (and identity) that you have internalized from a society that tells you that you are wrong.

Reference

Neves, S. (2021). *Compulsive sexual behaviors: A psycho-sexual treatment guide for clinicians*. Abingdon, Oxon: Routledge.

Chapter 2

Myths About Gay Men and Sex

Biases

Despite even our best intentions, we all have biases. They are impossible not to have. As mental health professionals, we need to be aware of our biases so that we decrease the risk of harming our clients. I would strongly recommend that anyone working with gay men take a Sexual Attitude Reassessment (SAR) class. It will provide you with exposure to aspects of sex that our clients may be into that you were unaware of and help you process your feelings around those behaviors. If you wrinkle your nose a bit or get a pit in your stomach about any of the below or do not know what a term means, you may especially want to consider a SAR. I have been through a SAR and an advanced SAR and learned a lot that was extremely helpful in my work.

A client mentions that he has to be meticulous about douching because he loves being fisted and wants to avoid a mud slide.

A client wants to be a total sub for his Daddy and his Daddy has asked him to bottom bareback, but he is not sure if he wants to take that risk.

A client shares that he is in a consensually non-monogamous relationship and wants to start fluid bonding with other guys, but his primary is not comfortable with that as an agreement.

A client is going to a circuit party and is trying to figure out a way to resist using G in order to hook up at an after-party.

A client is talking about how he could never tell his straight friends about his favorite parts of the bathhouse (the sex swing and watersports room) and how the sex is truly anonymous in parts of the bathhouse because it is too dark to see anything, let alone someone's face and body, and no one talks.

You do not have to be completely unphased or comfortable with any of the above. We all have our preferences and levels of discomfort. What you do need is to know how you feel about these behaviors, so that a face is not made or closed-off body language displayed by you in session without your

DOI: 10.4324/9781003386322-3

awareness. This could be shaming for the client. Your awareness of what you are experiencing and how you are reacting could allow you to address it for yourself internally, decreasing or eliminating the shame for the client. A great rule to live by is to not yuck someone else's yum. If you are not into something, that is fine, and do not shame or deprive someone else around it.

Sex Addiction? No! Compulsive Sexual Behaviors? Maybe

Gay men do tend, overall, to have more sex and sexual partners than their heterosexual peers. It is not uncommon for an uninformed therapist to consider a gay man having sex multiple times per week with multiple new partners a sex addict. It is not uncommon for gay men to feel that they are addicted to porn because they watch and masturbate numerous times a day. The truth is, there is not, inherently, anything wrong or unhealthy with either of these behaviors. Some people like to have sex multiple times a week with multiple different partners. Some people like to masturbate to porn and do not restrict it to once a day. Some people just like to live their lives in a way that feels natural and stimulating to them, while not hurting themselves or anyone around them (well, at least not without consent). It is easy to chalk up these atypical ways of going about sex as an addiction and use a 12-step program as an intervention. The truth is most sex therapists and educators do not prescribe to the idea of sex addiction.

"Research studies have continuously failed to prove that [sexual addiction] is a common condition or even that it exists at all" (Kort, 2018). And the American Association of Sexuality Educators, Counselors and Therapists' (AASECT) position is that while it understands that people can suffer consequences due to issues related to sex, it "...does not find sufficient empirical evidence to support the classification of sex addiction or porn addiction as a mental health disorder..." (AASECT.org, n.d.).

Let's stop pathologizing different desires or choices around sex. Let's stop telling people they need to stop watching porn. "It is now well documented that the biggest struggle that people face with porn isn't actually the watching it or masturbating to it, but the shame they feel about it" (Neves, 2021). Let's not pile more shame onto these individuals.

What we need to pay attention to and look to treat, if the client so desires, are compulsive sexual behaviors. Addiction is a diagnosable mental health disorder with very specific criteria that need to be met. Compulsive behaviors are those that a person tends to engage in without necessarily thinking and may have negative consequences. We will address the assessment and treatment of compulsive sexual behaviors in the intervention section of this book.

Anal Sex

During my SAR we watched a video clip of two men who were in a relationship having sex. What surprised a lot of my classmates, the majority of which were not gay men, was that the men in the clip did not have anal sex. I know that it is difficult to hear about gay men and sex in the media without the labels "tops" and "bottoms" being thrown around. And, yes, on all of the hookup apps you have an option to designate yourself as a top or bottom, or as versatile. Like many of my sexuality mentors, I believe a more accurate use of these words would be as verbs and not nouns, so that one tops or one bottoms. And, as was shown in the above-mentioned clip, topping and bottoming are often not even part of the sex. Oftentimes, partners take pleasure from a lot of other sexual acts outside of penetrative sex and plenty of gay men do not enjoy, or are not interested in, penetrative sex. Dr. Joe Kort has coined the term "side" to describe this option for gay men and hookup apps have started to add "side" as a labeling option, in addition to top, bottom, and versatile. You want to be open to the idea that sex for gay men does not need to include penetration and there are gay men who do have fulfilling sex lives without it.

Gay Men are More Likely to be Minor-Attracted People

Nope. While this is an idea that has been perpetuated by certain political bodies to discriminate against gay men, studies have shown that there is no correlation between one's sexual orientation and being sexually attracted to children or adolescents (LGBPsychology.org, n.d.). Are there gay men who fantasize about having sex with young boys or males with young-looking bodies? Of course, as do heterosexual men about young girls. If a gay male client brings up these types of fantasies, please do not automatically shame him, think him a child molester, or report him to the police. You need only report this person if these are fantasies that he intends to act on or has acted on. We can fantasize about whatever we want or even act those fantasies out in role plays with consenting adults. There is no harm in either.

Gay Men Just Can't Commit to Monogamy

Along with this idea that gay men just want to have a lot of sex is the notion that they cannot be monogamous. And if they try to, they will wind up cheating. The truth is, yes, gay men are more likely than their heterosexual counterparts to engage in consensual non-monogamous relationships (CNM). About 40% of gay couples reported being in sexually open/non-monogamous relationships (LaSala, 2004). This is not because they are too sex-starved to be with just one person. Since gay men are used to being a sexual minority, gay men are less encumbered by traditional and randomly decided heteronormative customs. Who is to say that monogamy is what should be strived for in a relationship? Who is to say that a relationship cannot be healthy and strong without monogamy? There are plenty of CNM relationships that are flourishing. It has been shown that relationship satisfaction did not differ between monogamous and openly non-monogamous gay male couples (LaSala, 2004). And, with 40% of gay men in sexually open/non-monogamous relationships, that leaves plenty of gay men who are monogamous. Please be careful not to pathologize gay men for being in CNM relationships, if that is what better fits their identities and needs, nor to assume that your gay male clients in monogamous relationships will not be able to stay monogamous.

References

AASECT.org (n.d.). Retrived, February 21, 2023 from https://www.aasect.org/position-sex-addiction

Kort, J. (2018). *LGBTQ clients in therapy: Clinical issues and treatment strategies.* New York, NY: W.W. Norton & Company.

LaSala, M.C. (2004). Extradyadic sex an gay male couples: Comparing monogamous and nonmonogamous relationships. *Families in Society, 85*(3), 405–412.

LGBPsychology.org (n.d.). Retrieved from https://lgbpsychology.org/html/facts_molestation.html#note1_text

Neves, S. (2021). *Compulsive sexual behaviors: A psycho-sexual treatment guide for clinicians.* Abingdon, Oxon: Routledge.

Chapter 3

Assessment for Sexual and Medical Issues

If something medical or physical is causing our client's sexual issue and we just give attention to their mental health needs, then we could be doing more harm than good. It is paramount that in addition to looking for the psychological causes of sexual issues, we also make sure to explore any potential medical causes and have them see a medical professional to explore those areas further.

Doctors Can Do More Harm

Please be aware that most doctors have their own hang-ups about discussing sexual issues, especially with gay men. And even if there was a level of comfort, the ability to treat is often lacking. Most medical school programs do not require classes on sexual health, and will often minimize its importance (Ross, Roth Bayer, Shindel, & Coleman, 2021). Also, most straight doctors have been shown to have strong implicit preferences for straight patients over gay male patients, which could contribute to disparities in care (Sabin, Riskind, & Nosek, 2015). So, you cannot just send your gay male clients to any doctor and expect them to get the care they need and deserve.

As can be imagined, this danger is amplified for gay men of color, persons with disabilities, and members of the transgender and non-binary communities. Gay Black men have been shown to have "prior experiences of, or anticipated negative interactions with, physicians and skepticism about the healthcare system" (Quinn, Dickson-Gomez, Zarwell, Pearson, & Lewis, 2019, p. 1959). Mulcahy et al. (2022) showed that, even with insurance, 40% of their disabled study participants reported that in the past 12 months the healthcare system managed to fail them in getting at least one healthcare need met. Seelman, Colon-Diaz, LeCroix, Xavier-Brier, and Kattari (2017) speak to how "healthcare services are rife with issues of discrimination and noninclusive care from doctors, clinicians, and staff" (p. 18) for transgender clients, which leads to "unequal treatment compared with patients who are not transgender" (p. 18). And a study looking at transgender and non-binary

DOI: 10.4324/9781003386322-4

youth who wanted gender-affirming care found there were major difficulties in finding a competent provider (Kearns, Kroll, O'Shea, & Neff, 2021).

Best-Kept Secrets of Medications

Since most doctors are not comfortable talking about sex, they do not tend to volunteer issues around sex when talking to clients about medication side effects. So, please be aware that the most popular medications for depression and anxiety, selective serotonin reuptake inhibitors (SSRIs), all have the potential for sexual side effects. SSRIs allow serotonin to stay around longer in the brain and serotonin contributes to less desire to have sex. Also, the mood stabilizer Lamictal has a small chance of sexual side effects, most atypical anti-psychotics (like Risperdal and Haldol) also behave like SSRIs (in addition to decreasing dopamine and increasing prolactin which tends to interfere with sex), and (as of the time of this writing) there is little known about how specific anti-anxiety medications and stimulants effect sex.

Assessing for Medical Contributors

When exploring possible medical or physiological issues, you will want to know whether they have had this issue for as long as they can remember, or if it started at a particular point in their life? If the former, then that does tend to lean more toward a non-psychological issue. If the latter, you will want to know what occurred during this point in their life. Was it a life stressor, major life change, or something physical or medically related? Certain operations and hundreds of medications (more detail on medication in Chapter 11) will cause sexual issues. Such surgeries include prostate surgery, bowel or rectal surgery, bladder removal, surgery to remove testicles, and surgery to remove lymph nodes from the back of the abdomen. You will also want to know if they have this issue when they are masturbating or only with a sexual partner or partners. If the issue is only occurring when they have sex with others, then that is more likely to be a psychological issue. If it is an erection issue, you will want to know if they are erect when they wake up, spontaneously throughout the day, or when they masturbate? If they can achieve an erection during any of these times, then it is less likely that this is a medical or physiological issue.

Regardless of what you find when asking these questions, you always want to rule out medical or physiological causes, working with your clients to find a competent and affirming doctor.

References

Kearns, S., Kroll, T., O'Shea, D., & Neff, K. (2021). Experiences of transgender and non-binary youth accessing gender-affirming care: A systematic review and meta ethnography. *Plos One, 16,* 1–29.

Mulcahy, A., Streed Jr., C.G., Wallisch, A., Batza, K., Kurth, N., Hall, J.P., & Jones McMaughan, D. (2022). Gender identity, disability, and unmet healthcare needs among disabled people living in the community in the United States. *International Journal of Environmental Research and Public Health, 19*, 2588–2607.

Quinn, K., Dickson-Gomez, J., Zarwell, M., Pearson, B., & Lewis, M. (2019). "A gay man and a doctor are just like, a recipe for destruction": How racism and homonegativity in healthcare settings influence PrEP uptake among young Black MSM. *AIDS and Behavior, 23*, 1951–1963.

Ross, M.W., Roth Bayer, C., Shindel, A., & Coleman, E. (2021). Evaluating the impact of a medical school cohort sexual health course on knowledge, counseling skills and sexual attitude change. *BMC Medical Education, 21*(37), 1–10.

Sabin, J.A., Riskind, R.G., & Nosek, B.A. (2015). Health care providers' implicit and explicit attitudes toward lesbian women and gay men. *American Journal of Public Health, 105*(9), 1831–1841.

Seelman, K.L., Colon-Diaz, M.J.P., LeCroix, R.H., Xavier-Brier, M., & Kattari, L. (2017). Transgender noninclusive healthcare and delaying care because of fear: Connections to general health and mental health among transgender adults. *Transgender Health, 2*(1), 17–28.

Chapter 4

Mental and Sexual Health Issues

A Traumatic Childhood Development

"Fag! Get away from us little gay boy! No one wants you around, sissy, go kill yourself!" Most gay boys have heard these words, or versions of these words, at least once in their lives. For far too many, these are words heard every day, often from their school peers, sometimes from their siblings, and sometimes from their own parents. And if no one in their personal life is saying these things to them, they only need to watch the news to see that they belong to an undesired group that people do not want to treat equally. How can any adult feel good about themselves and what they have to offer others (including in respect of something as vulnerable as sex) when messaging like the above has been internalized and hardwired into their brains. How likely is it for a "fag" or "sissy", that no one wants around, to feel confident going into sexual situations?

Gay boys and adolescents experience another disadvantage when it comes to having them feel comfortable with sex later in life. If their parents did talk to them about the birds and bees, they likely did not talk about sex between two men. If their school had a sexual education class, it very likely did not mention that there are other forms of sex than between a man and a woman. It is rare that they will be asked which one of the boys in their school they have a crush on or want to be their boyfriend. Gay boys and adolescents, like all human beings, long for an intimate connection with others. But imagine the toll of having to keep these natural desires a secret, or even going against your true nature and pretending you like girls, simply in order to fit in and feel safe. Imagine being denied the practice and trial and error around dating, relationships, and sex. Growing up this way, it is difficult to avoid the likelihood that sex as an adult with other men will involve some form of shame.

Ambivalent Attachment Style

Growing up in this way, obviously, has negative consequences when it comes to what style of attachment gay men tend to develop. Allan (2022) points

DOI: 10.4324/9781003386322-5

specifically to 1) the roles of peers, 2) coming out, and 3) homophobia, heterosexism, and homonegative messaging contributing to gay boys having difficulties in their development. For most of my gay male clients I have seen these same elements contribute to an ambivalent attachment style. Accordingly, when it comes to adult intimate relationships, individuals will have a preoccupation with the availability of the attachment figure and intense distress when there is separation from the attachment figure (Wallin, 2007). I have often seen this preoccupation lead to anxieties related to sex with their partner/attachment figure. Since they feel their sense of safety hinges on having their partner around, then, naturally, it will seem dire that they perform or please that partner sexually in order to keep them around. This often increases sexual issues due to increased performance anxiety and decreased attention to whether or not they themselves are receiving pleasure from sex.

Systems Are to Blame

I hope you are seeing that the added stressors experienced by gay men are not created internally; rather, they come from a society that fears what is unknown to them, so looks to oppress others in order to feel safer and better about themselves. This subjugating happens on a systems level, from the most intimate (family members) to the most top-level (government policies and laws).

Iasenza (2020) speaks to Heinz Kohut's term of gleam in the mother's eye (an ability of the caregiver to be nurturing, empathetic, and connected to the child) as a necessary factor in children developing a healthy relationship to desire and how "if LGBTQ people are lucky enough to experience caregivers with a degree of 'gleams of the eye' in general, many still experience familial and/or societal absence of mirroring non-normative sexual and gender experience" (p. 148). This leaves all members of the LGBTQ+ community at a likely disadvantage when it comes to a very early and fundamental stage of building healthy desire.

The increased chance of being shunned at school, in their neighborhood, in their state, and by entire countries takes its toll – lesbian, gay, and bisexual youth are four times more likely to attempt suicide than heterosexual youth (American Psychiatric Association, 2017). And communities are even harsher to Black, Indigenous, and People of Color (BIPOC) LGBTQ+ communities. A qualitative study by Ghabrial (2014) found that LGBTQ people of color experienced "feelings of disconnect from both the larger sexual minority community, as well as their ethnoracial community" (p. 17), that they have conflictual feelings about their multiple identities, and that they feel pressure from their LGBTQ communities to come out to their friends and family from traditionally homophobic cultures. Nadal (2013) speaks to the increased microaggressions that LGBTQ people of color must deal with, which greatly impact their mental health, and also to the higher violent crimes committed against this community. Transgender Black women are especially prone to being targeted for violence and murder. McGuffey (2018) found that the Black LGBT participants in their study experienced substantial "discrimination between and within various raced, sexualized, and gendered groups" (p. 461). American Indian and Alaskan Natives also experience high levels of discrimination and those reporting severe levels of bias-related victimization were also more likely to report depression, anxiety, and substance abuse issues (Parker, Duran, & Walters, 2017).

Another community facing increased oppression due to systems are older gay men. Perone, Ingersoll-Dayton, and Watkins-Dukhie (2020) point to how "decades of historical trauma and discrimination have left many LGBTQ + older adults more vulnerable to social isolation and loneliness" (p. 137); to compound this, "LGBTQ+ resources focus on youth, and many aging resources focus on the needs of heterosexual, cisgender older adults, which leaves LGBTQ+ older adults in a quandary of where to find cultur-ally appropriate services" (p. 136). Not only do they lack support in com-munities in which they once thrived, but data show that once they start entering care facilities, the inadequate level of care they encounter in these environments contribute to them suffering from depression and anxiety (Tinney et al., 2015).

And if you are a gay male and transgender, asexual, kinky, disabled, or non-binary then you are further ostracized from your community. Su et al. (2016) showed that compared "to nontransgender respondents, transgen-der individuals were at higher odds of reporting discrimination, depres-sion symptoms, and attempted suicides" (p. 18). And Timmins, Rimes, and Rahman (2020) were able to show a link between prejudice events and distress when it came to gender non-conformity. It has also been shown that asexual individuals face greater negative bias and prejudice from het-erosexual people than do other sexual minorities (Bauer, Kaye, & Brotto, 2020). Rothblum, Krueger, Kittle, and Meyer (2020) showed that asexual lesbian, gay, bisexual, gender queer, or non-binary individuals "reported feeling more stigma than non-asexual men and women" (p. 765), suggest-ing that "asexual identity is more stigmatized in society than LGB sexual minority identities" (p. 765). For kinksters, society's stigma related to bondage, discipline/domination, sadism/submission, and masochism (BDSM) play often discourages them from accepting and engaging in their desires (Hebert & Weaver, 2015), and this shame can lead to poorer mental health. For example, BDSM-identifying individuals have a higher risk of suicide when compared to non-BDSM-identifying individuals (Cramer et al., 2017), due to societal discrimination. And since we live in an ableist society, persons with disabilities continue to struggle to get locations and services to meet their needs and to be seen as valid human beings of worth. Kattari (2020) found that, regardless of the type of disability or impairment, all persons with disabilities experienced high levels of ableist microaggressions.

Duncan and Hatzenbuehler (2014) speak to the role environment plays in the mental health of the overall LGBTQ community by showing that for "sexual minority adolescents, suicidal ideation and suicide attempts were significantly more likely to occur in neighborhoods with a greater prevalence of LGBT assault hate crimes" (p. 276). Hatzenbuehler, Keyes, and Hasin (2009) found that state-level policies that do not legally protect lesbian, gay, and bisexual rights are tied to "psychiatric disorders, particularly generalized anxiety disorder and post-traumatic stress disorder, as well as dysthymia" (p. 2278). And Mustanski, Birkett, Greene, Hatzenbuehler, and Newcomb (2014) were able to show that lesbian, gay, and bisexual health is affected by high-level policies. This is because since "people are often highly dependent on their institutions to protect or support them, violations of trust may compound the effects of difficult or traumatic experiences" (Drabble et al., 2019, p. 497). And I have no doubt that this connection between policies and mental health is also true for transgender and gender nonbinary individuals. For example, Drabble et al. (2019) found that after the 2016 election, concerns were most increased among transgender and gender non-conforming groups. They also found, post-election, that their sample (sexual minority women and/or transgender or gender non-conforming individuals) felt less safe, more concerned about continuing to be protected in states that they had previously felt support from, and increased worry for others in less supportive states.

Individuals from these groups are internalizing these added stressors and self-confidence crushing movements to take away their rights and not treat them as equal human beings. This affects every aspect of the lives of gay men, including how they think about and experience sex. "The family, relationship, and sexual histories of…gay men often can contain additional sources of sexual guilt, anxiety, and shame due to societal and internalized homophobia" (Iasenza, 2020). And society also plays a large role in the kind of sex most gay men wind up having. Odets (2019) coined the term "sports sex" to refer to sex that gay men have which tends to be devoid of emotion and more about performance. Because so many gay boys grow up believing that romance is not for them, and that romance was only being reserved for straight boys and girls, they will sperate their sex from emotional feelings and therefore miss out on the connecting to others and the self-discovery that can happen through emotionally connected sex (Odets, 2019).

References

Allan, R. (2022). We cannot change what we cannot see ourselves: Integrating attachment theory into couple therapy with gay men. In R. Harvey, M.J. Murphy, J.J. Bigner, & J.L. Wetchler (Eds.), *Handbook of LGBTQ-Affirmative couple and family therapy*. New York, NY: Routledge.

American Psychiatric Association. (2017). *Mental health disparities: LGBTQ*. Washington, DC: Division of Diversity and Health Equity.

Bauer, C., Kaye, S.L., & Brotto, L.A. (2020). Understanding alcohol and tobacco consumption in asexual samples: A mixed-methods approach (asexual and nonasexual). *Archives of Sexual Behavior, 49*, 733–755.

Cramer, R.J., Mandracchia, T.M., Holley, S.R., Wright, S., Moody, K., & Nobles, M.R. (2017). Can need for affect and sexuality differentiate suicide risk in three community samples? *Journal of Social and Clinical Psychology, 36*(8), 704–722.

Drabble, L.A., Veldhuis, C.B., Wootton, A., Riggle, E.D.B., & Hughes, T.L. (2019). Mapping the landscape of support and safety among sexual minority women and gender non-conforming individuals: Perceptions after the 2016 US presidential election. *Sexuality Research and Social Policy, 16*, 488–500.

Duncan, D.T., & Hatzenbuehler, M.L. (2014). Lesbian, gay, bisexual, and transgender hate crimes and suicidality among a population-based sample of sexual-minority adolescents in Boston. *American Journal of Public Health, 104*(2), 272–278.

Ghabrial, M. (2014). *"Trying to figure out where we belong": Narratives of racialized sexual minorities on community, identity, discrimination, and health*. Retrieved from ProQuest LLC. (10185633)

Hatzenbuehler, M.L., Keyes, K.M., & Hasin, D.S. (2009). State-Level policies and psychiatric morbidity in lesbian, gay, and bisexual populations. *American Journal of Public Health, 99*(12), 2275–2281.

Hebert, A., & Weaver, A. (2015). Perks, problems, and the people who play: A qualitative exploration of dominant and submissive BDSM roles. *The Canadian Journal of Human Sexuality, 24*(1), 49–62.

Iasenza, S. (2020). *Transforming sexual narratives: A relational approach to sex therapy*. New York, NY: Routledge.

Kattari, S.K. (2020). Ableist microaggressions and the mental health of disabled adults. *Community Mental Health Journal, 56*, 1170–1179.

McGuffey, C.S. (2018). Intersectionality, cognition, disclosure and Black LGBT views on civil rights and marriage equality. *DuBois Review, 15*(2), 441–465.

Mustanski, B., Birkett, M., Greene, G.J., Hatzenbuehler, M.L., & Newcomb, M.E. (2014). Envisioning an America without sexual orientation inequities in adolescent health. *American Journal of Public Health, 104*(2), 218–224.

Nadal, K. (2013). *That's so gay!: Microaggressions and the lesbian, gay, bisexual, and transgender community*. Washington, DC: American Psychological Association.

Odets, W. (2019). *Out of the shadows: Reimagining gay men's lives*. New York, NY: Picador.

Parker, M., Duran, B., & Walters, K. (2017). The relationship between bias-related victimization and generalized anxiety disorder among American Indian and

Alaska Native lesbian, gay, bisexual, transgender, two-spirit community members. *International Journal of Indigenous Health*, *12*(2), 64–83.

Perone, A.K., Ingersoll-Dayton, B., & Watkins-Dukhie, K. (2020). Social isolation loneliness among LGBT older adults: Lessons learned from a pilot friendly caller program. *Clinical Social Work Journal*, *48*, 126–139.

Rothblum, E.D., Krueger, E.A., Kittle, K.R., & Meyer, I.H. (2020). Asexual and non-asexual respondents from a U.S. population-based study of sexual minorities. *Archives of Sexual Behavior* (2020) *49*, 757–767.

Su, D., Irwin, J.A., Fisher, C., Ramos, A., Kelley, M., Rogel Mendoza, D.A., & Coleman, J.D. (2016). Mental health disparities within the LGBT population: A comparison between transgender and nontransgender individuals. *Transgender Health*, *1*(1), 12–20.

Timmins, L., Rimes, K.A., & Rahman, Q. (2020). Minority stressors, rumination, and psychological distress in lesbian, gay, and bisexual individuals. *Archives of Sexual Behavior*, *49*, 661–680.

Tinney, J., Dow, B., Maude, P., Purchase, R., Whyte, C., & Barrett, C. (2015). Mental health issues and discrimination among older LGBTI people. *International Psychogeriatrics*, *27*(9), 1411–1416.

Wallin, D. J. (2007). *Attachment in psychotherapy*. New York, NY: The Guilford Press.

Chapter 5

Body Issues

External Validation Needs and Toxic Masculinity – A Dangerous Combination

Recall that child I showed growing up assaulted with hateful messaging? What are the chances that this child feels good about themselves at their core? What are the chances the adult they grow up to be has honed the ability to internally validate themselves? Not very high. Downs (2012) speaks to how, because of the lack of experience in providing themselves with internal validation, gay men wind up running "roughshod over the subtleties that lie with us, and choose instead to grab at the nearest and brightest flag that will draw attention and, hopefully, validation of the world around us" (p. 77). Gay men wind up searching outside themselves to experience validation, because we all need some form of validation to feel good about ourselves. When you combine this dire need for external validation with toxic masculinity for gay men, you wind up with a lot of men who feel that they must get their external validation by showing, through their bodies, just how masculine they really are. Toxic masculinity is a very real phenomenon for gay men. Joe Kort (2018) points out that since gay men "are punished from childhood for their natural desire to be softer and gentler and have romantic feelings for another male" (p. 109) and experience a history of being called derogatory effeminate taunts, "it is no wonder that some gay men go to such extremes to project a masculine identity" (p. 110) which may not be congruent with their true sense of masculinity. This concept of men disregarding their true sense of masculinity in a defense against being seen as feminine is supported by Glick, Gangl, Gibb, Klumpner, and Weinberg's (2007) study in which participants who were randomly told that they had scored high on femininity on a personality test "exhibited increased negative affect toward effeminate but not toward masculine gay men" (p. 57). These men being told just once, by what they thought was a personality test, that they were effeminate was enough to have them be more likely to act out toward femininity in other men. Sanchez and Vilain (2012) also provide evidence that

DOI: 10.4324/9781003386322-6

"gay men wished to be more masculine and less feminine than they perceived themselves to be" (p. 117). In the gay male world, this presentation of masculinity tends to play out in two very specific ways. Either you are extremely muscular (a six-pack, a large, defined, and rock-hard chest, and bulging biceps and triceps – the focus tends to be on the upper body, so you can skip a leg day at the gym) or a Paul Bunyan of a man, which in the community is affectionately referred to as a bear or cub. Bears are allowed to be fat and cubs chubby; however, each still needs a large upper torso and, preferably, a hairy face and body. I would say these are two out of the three specific body types that are most celebrated and accepted within the gay male community. The third seems to embody the gay male's desire to preserve youth, being very slim, hairless, tight, and firm. These men are known as twinks and I believe that often (but not always) they are sought out by gay men to accentuate their own masculinity in comparison.

Having just three cherished body types, pushes so many gay men to feel like they must fit into one of these categories and leaves most gay men not fitting into any of them. And even in the cases of the gay men who have these preferred body types: 1) because external validation is so important, they will often feel as if their bodies could always fit the stereotype even more or 2) they will feel they have to adhere to the traits and characteristics of those stereotypes, even if it is not actually their identity. Between the gay men that do not happen to have one of the preferred body presentations, those that do but feel a need to strive for a "better" body, and those feeling their body presentation is incongruent with their identity, you have a lot of gay men entering scenarios where they get naked in front of another man and feel shame about their bodies. They often feel as if they do not "measure up".

Additional Hardships for Those Further Marginalized

Speaking of "measuring up", in addition to the above pressures, Black men are expected to have extremely large penises – the term BBC (Big Black Cock) being very well known in the gay male community. Similarly, Latin men are expected to be hairy, aggressive papis (daddies), also with large penises. And Asians are expected to be slim and not sexual at all – Nadal (2013) speaks to the "invisibility and desexualization of Asian American men" (p. 115).

Other groups that tend to be told that they should be devoid of sexuality are persons with disabilities and/or chronic illness and the aging. Those with disabilities and/or chronic illness often have trouble seeing themselves as sexual beings because their bodies do not match up with society's messaging around what a sexual body should look like. This can easily lead to having a fear of engaging in, or not feeling deserving of, sex. For many people within this community, their biggest hurdle to sex is feeling like sexual beings and once they can see themselves this way, they tend to be able to figure out how to make sex work for them (Kaufman, Silverberg, & Odette, 2007). Gay aging males suffer a similar hardship, often being told that they are "too old" for sex. And to make matters worse, the idea of "too old" starts much earlier in the gay male community than in the heterosexual community. For example, there is a popular gay porn site called "Men Over 30" which defines itself as a site that "features older hot men…".

And what about taking off one's clothes and engaging in sex for individuals who are transgender, non-binary, or queer (TGNBQ)? Some uneducated sexual partners or sexual partners unfamiliar with transgender and non-binary bodies misname their genitals, focus more on the TGNBQ individual's genitals than the TGNBQ individual is comfortable with, and have preconceived notions of what is supposed to be done to their genitals during sex (Fielding, 2021). Even before engaging in a sexual act, a lot of TGNBQ people experience dysphoria; this often keeps them from feeling good enough about their body to enter into a sexual situation.

References

Downs, A. (2012). *The velvet rage: Overcoming the pain of growing up gay in a straight man's world.* Boston, MA: Da Capo Press.

Fielding, L. (2021). *Trans sex: Clinical approaches to trans sexualities and erotic embodiments.* New York, NY: Routledge.

Glick, P., Gangl, C., Gibb, S. & Klumpner, S., & Weinberg, E. (2007). Defensive reactions to masculinity threat: More negative affect toward effeminate (but not masculine) gay men. *Sex Roles, 57*, 55–59.

Kaufman, M., Silverberg, C., & Odette, F. (2007). *The ultimate guide to sex and disability: For all of us who live with disabilities, chronic pain, and illness.* San Francisco, CA: Cleis Press, Inc.

Kort, J. (2018). *LGBTQ clients in therapy: Clinical issues and treatment strategies.* New York, NY: W.W. Norton & Company.

Nadal, K. (2013). *That's so gay! Microaggressions and the lesbian, gay, bisexual, and transgender community.* Washington, DC: American Psychological Association.

Sanchez, F.J., & Vilain, E. (2012). "Straight-acting gays": The relationship between masculine consciousness, anti-effeminacy, and negative gay identity. *Archives of Sexual Behavior, 41*, 111–119.

Chapter 6

Anxiety

Why Gay Men Are More Likely to Experience Anxiety

Due to discrimination, stigma, emotional and physical abuse, microaggressions, living through the AIDS epidemic, persecution, and constant messaging that they are less than human, it is no wonder that gay men experience higher stress levels than their heterosexual counterparts. Bostwick, Boyd, Hughes, and McCabe (2010) showed in their study that 41% of gay men had a lifetime prevalence of any anxiety disorder, while the same was true for 19% of heterosexual men. And if you are gay and aging, you have the added stress of likely being discriminated against at aged care settings (Tinney et al., 2015). "At a vulnerable age they are also asked, overtly and/or covertly to 'un-queer' themselves and surrender, suppress, and deny their queer identity in order to fit into heteronormative, white-centric expectations and settings" (Levatino, 2022, p. 328). Those aged care settings tend to be filled with non-queer elders who can be very homophobic and racist and even within queer communities, queer elders tend to be excluded, especially non-white elders (Levatino, 2022).

Also, unsurprisingly, the more ableist microaggressions a person with disabilities experiences, the more likely they are to also experience poorer mental health outcomes, including anxiety (Kattari, 2020). And gay men who also belong to a race/ethnicity minority group are even more likely to experience stress, due to the discrimination around their race/ethnicity (Zamboni & Crawford, 2005).

It has also been shown that transgender and gender-diverse populations are more likely to meet the criteria for an anxiety disorder than cisgender individuals (Stanton et al., 2021). When it comes to sex and stress, "Genitalia are a (if not the *the*) prime signifier of sex and sexuality, so [those] having bodies that do not simply match that gender identity is often a source of distress" (Lev & Sennott, 2022, p. 156). Oftentimes, transgender, non-binary, and/or queer (TGNBQ) individuals have great anxiety around what is going to happen when they reveal their bodies for sex and intimacy, even if they

DOI: 10.4324/9781003386322-7

have already shared how their naked bodies will appear. They worry about rejection, violence, or even being killed. These are their realities. And even when not choosing to reveal their bodies, others choose to make their genitalia a subject of discussion. Many people feel they have the right to ask TGNBQ individuals about their genitalia, casually asking whether they have had surgeries and whether they have a penis or a vulva. This type of questioning would cause anxiety even for a person who society deems has the "right" genitals, so imagine the impact it has on TGNBQ individuals.

How Anxiety Negatively Affects Sex

While you want some anxiety to make sex hot, it can very easily overwhelm and lead to plenty of sexual issues. Anxiety easily puts us into survival mode and when in survival mode our brain accesses its most primitive parts and does whatever it deems necessary to keep us alive, even if our life is not actually in danger. When prioritizing and focusing on personal survival (for example, flight, fight, freeze, or fawn), sex is at the very bottom of the list of what will keep us alive in the moment (Nagoski, 2015). So, even feeling slight stress could lower our desire for sex, distract us from being present for sex, or interfere with our sexual activities. Two common examples of manifestations for gay men of anxiety during sex are the sphincter tightening up during receptive anal sex and issues getting or maintaining an erection.

While I have discussed the many issues that do add to unique stressors for gay men that could wind up being brought into the bedroom, there is a stressor for gay men that happens because the sex itself is happening between men. Because of growing up being so worried about seeming "needy, feminine, or 'sissy'" (p. 13) some gay men have trouble as adults being vulnerable and having intimacy with other men (Greenan & Tunnell, 2003). Sex puts gay men in vulnerable positions that may take away from seeing themselves as masculine enough, creating great anxiety.

References

Bostwick, W.B., Boyd, C.J., Hughes, T.L., & McCabe, S.E. (2010). Dimensions of sexual orientation and the prevalence of mood and anxiety disorders in the United States. *Research and Practice Journal*, *100*(3), 468–475.

Greenan, D., & Tunnell, G. (2003). *Couple therapy with gay men*. New York: The Guilford Press.

Kattari, S.K. (2020). Ableist microaggressions and the mental health of disabled adults. *Community Mental Health Journal*, *56*, 1170–1179.

Lev, A.I., & Sennott, S.L. (2022). Sexuality and desire landscapes in transgender, nonbinary, and genderqueer relationships. In R. Harvey, M.J. Murphy, J.J. Bigner, & J.L. Wetchler (Eds.), *Handbook of LGBTQ-affirmative couple and family therapy*. New York, NY: Routledge.

Levatino, P.D. (2022). "I didn't know I had a right to exist": Queer elders and family therapy. In R. Harvey, M.J. Murphy, J.J. Bigner, & J.L. Wetchler (Eds.), *Handbook of LGBTQ-Affirmative couple and family therapy*. New York, NY: Routledge.

Nagoski, E. (2015). *Come as you are: The surprising new science that will transform your sex life*. New York, NY: Simon & Schuster Paperbacks.

Stanton, A.M., Batchelder, A.W., Kirakosian, N., Scholl, J., King, D, Grasso, C., Potter, J., Mayer, K.H., & Cleirigh, C.O. (2021). Differences in mental health symptom severity and care engagement among transgender and gender diverse individuals: Findings from a larger community health center. *PLoS One*, *16*(1), 1–15.

Tinney, J., Dow, B., Maude, P., Purchase, R., Whyte, C. & Barrett, C. (2015). Mental health issues and discrimination among older LGBTI people. *International Psychogeriatrics*, *27*(9), 1411–1416.

Zamboni, B.D., & Crawford, I. (2005). Minority stress and sexual problems among African-American gay and bisexual men. *Archives of Sexual Behavior*, *36*, 569–578.

Chapter 7

Depression and Substance Abuse

As a Puerto Rican child, when I was teased about my ethnicity at school, I would go home and see my family, who were also Puerto Rican, not living up to the stereotypes that were being thrown at me. I could also go directly to my mother, let her know what was happening to me, and be reassured that being Puerto Rican did not make me a bad person. I suffered a completely different experience when I was teased and bullied for being gay. I could not look at my family for evidence to go against what my schoolmates were saying about me and I, in no way, felt comfortable enough telling my mother what was happening. I dealt with this shame all on my own, so it just continued to build. Greenan and Tunnell (2003) share how gay youth typically "cannot depend on their families to be a safe harbor from the homophobic prejudice of the outside world" (p. 5).

The Greater Shame Gay Men Experience

I have yet to work with a gay male client who has not felt some degree of internalized heterosexism. You might be wondering if I meant to say internalized "homophobia." In my opinion, the term internalized heterosexism is a more accurate representation of what my clients experience. Many are not afraid, or phobic, of their gay identity. Instead, they experience shame because of how they are treated by a heterosexist society. We live in a society where most of the beliefs and content we take in promotes heterosexism as the ideal. It's impossible to live in this kind of world without having some shame for *not* being heterosexual. Robbins (2018) found that internalized heterosexism leads to shame, and this shame results in increased depression. Our society also tends to be threatened by, and does not value, genders that are not cisgender or part of the binary, sex that is not vanilla, and attraction that does not involve sex. This leads gender and sexual minorities overall to internalize some sense of shame because of how they are seen and treated by society.

DOI: 10.4324/9781003386322-8

That shame and depression will often get in the way of someone being able to be in a place internally where they can derive pleasure from sex. For gay men, there is shame that is also related directly to sex. In the United States, sex is not to be discussed between parents and children or even between partners. Most parents are reluctant to have "the talk" with their children and most intimate partners just expect magic to happen during sex, without talking about sex before, during, and after the act. This sense of taboo gets intensified when it comes to gay boys. While, in our society, sex is generally kept secretive, for gay males it is considered "dirty", from childhood through adulthood. When parents do talk about sex with their children, this typically involves discussion of sex between a man and woman. When children watch television shows or movies, romance and sex is typically between a man and a woman. And children learn early on that boys should like and kiss girls, not boys. This makes what gay boys would actually want to do, be intimate with another boy, seem dirty or wrong. This way of seeing it will keep some gay boys from pursuing something so natural and pleasurable. Some gay boys will go for it anyway, with great fear. Fear of being caught by adults doing something that is "wrong" and fear of great losses and/or violence. Whether the child decides to pursue or just keep their desires to themselves, the secrecy is still there, and shame thrives on secrecy. And this shame does not just disappear after childhood.

Plenty of our gay male clients did not grow up in the age of hookup apps. Gay men do not have the luxury of being able to assume that every guy they meet, be it at work or at a restaurant, is likely also gay, nor the privilege of taking the risk of coming out to others if they did not know if the other person is also gay. And even gay bars did not always offer a safe place to meet. During the 19th and 20th centuries, gay bars (where gay men were just socializing with each other) were raided by the police, religious institutions, and the Mafia, with the patrons being outed and the bars being shut down. For men to enjoy the natural behavior of sex, they often had to go to areas of parks known to gay men for meeting other men with whom to have sex – so-called "cruising" areas. And this was not some sweet picnic scene. This was typically at night/in the dark, with guys barely saying a word to each other (before, during, or after sex), eyeing each other to assess interest, and then most likely having sex there or going somewhere else a bit more private, albeit likely still public, for sex. Such places might include a public restroom, a bath house, or the dark backroom of a gay bar. Places that were all objectively dirty and dangerous. Dangerous not only because of the possible violence that may occur in these public areas, but also because plain-clothed police officers would routinely pretend to be interested in sex with men in these places and then arrest the men they had just entrapped. Please understand that I do not begrudge or judge people who want to have sex in these ways. What I am trying to make clear is that gay men did not have the same options as their heterosexual counterparts, even when it came to sex in the privacy of their own home. In some states in the United States, sex between two men was actually illegal. It is only since the beginning of the 21st century that sodomy laws in the United States have finally been removed from the statute book. Imagine the effect of being told that the kind of sex you have is so unnatural that it is actually against the law.

While there are no longer sodomy laws, there continues to be a hyper-fixation of heterosexual people seeing gay male sex as appalling, so the shame for gay men is still ever-present. A 2021 study by Ray and Parkhill found, for a sample of over 400 heterosexual men, "that gay men's sexual behavior is the most likely elicitor of disgust and antigay hostility, as opposed to a perceived pathogen threat or moral transgression" (p. 1). This fixation tends to be especially strong among those who are religious. Wilkinson and Roys (2005) found in their study "that as participants' religiosity scores increased, their impressions of the gay behavioral target (reading about the gay man's sexual history versus their fantasies or attractions) became more negative" (p. 71).

"Hate the sin, not the sinner" is a common trope that gets thrown at gay men to explain how certain religions are accepting of them, as long as they do behave the natural way most gay men do and have sex with other men. So, the message is that you can be who you are, but you cannot act on any of the behaviors that naturally go along with who you are (especially having sex); if you indulge in those behaviors, then you are a sinner. And, for most religions, this is the most generous of messaging as it relates to gay men. Most gay men grew up in households with parents and siblings practicing and living by a religion that told them they were evil because they desired to have sex with other men. This messaging is likely to be even more pervasive for gay men of color. It has been shown that "LGB individuals of color were more likely to affiliate with a non-affirming religious institution" (Johnson, Rostosky, & Riggle, 2022, p. 348). Regardless of race or ethnicity, a lot of gay men grew up in religious households where conversion therapy was a real option the family would want the child to pursue if they came out as gay. Research has shown conversion therapy to be very harmful and unethical. Jenkins and Johnson (2004) show "that seeking to change a person's sexual orientation may cause irreparable psychological, emotional, and spiritual harm" (p. 561). As of this writing, only 20 states in the U.S., as well as Washington, D.C., have a statewide law banning conversion therapy for minors (Movement Advancement Project, 2022). It is clear that growing up in religious households and with larger institutions telling you are evil for wanting to and/or having sex with another man will interfere with your ability to take pleasure from sex with another man.

As mentioned in Chapter 1, the AIDS crisis forever joined sex for gay men with fear and shame because of how society branded and treated those with HIV and AIDS. It is also worth noting that for years during the beginning of the AIDS epidemic, no reliable HIV test was available. This meant that gay men were living for years in ignorance of whether or not they had something inside them that would soon kill them and also any potential partner. Many men during this time just assumed that they must be HIV+ and would soon be dying. Odets (2019) speaks to the survivors of this period experiencing an:

> Ongoing psychological aftermath of an uncontrolled, deeply stigmatizing fifteen-year plague that resulted in a third of a million deaths in our relatively small, long-stigmatized gay community. Many of the surviving men…are, in the strictest sense of the idea, survivors of trauma. At the very least, they are survivors of extraordinary, accumulated loss, which is itself a trauma.
>
> (pp. 15–16)

This is yet another experience unique to gay men that contributes to depression and taints sex.

Increased Isolation for Gay Men

Depression being so prevalent for gay men means that often gay men are also lonely men. There are so many obstacles that society puts in place to keep gay men isolated: a childhood of having no one to turn to when being mistreated by family, peers, and society; an adolescence of being discouraged from forming romantic relationships; and an adulthood of staying to themselves to avoid shame and violence, and then feeling shame for being so isolated (Odets, 2019). "For someone who feels unwanted or contemptable, isolation is safety" (Odets, 2019, p. 157). Humans are social beings, and we need connection, we need a tribe. Imagine the horror of wanting to be around others, but feeling you are better off just staying by yourself, and thus experiencing the pain of loneliness.

One group within gay men that face an especially difficult experience of loneliness are the aging. Perone, Ingersoll-Dayton, and Watkins-Dukhie (2020) point to how "decades of historical trauma and discrimination have left many LGBTQ + older adults more vulnerable to social isolation and loneliness" (p. 137) . The lack of support is a critical issue for this population because they tend to have less family support than their non-queer counterparts. Additionally, the queer community they once counted on will likely no longer be there for them due to ageism. Nadal (2013) states how a lack of support from the LGBT community could be especially painful for aging LGBT individuals because many from this generation endured so much to gain rights that the younger generations (who are ignoring them) now get to freely enjoy. Not only do they lack support in communities in which they once thrived, data show that once they start entering care facilities, the inadequate care for queer people in these environments contributes to them suffering from depression and anxiety (Tinney et al., 2015).

Most care homes are a dangerous and lonely place for queer individuals. Simpson, Almack, and Walthery's (2018) assessment of care homes showed that, while they found favorable attitudes from staff on LGBT issues, their knowledge of LGBT issues was not well-developed, training around LGBT care issues was low, there was no effort to identify which residents were LGBT (so many were further marginalized by being seen as heterosexual or cisgender), and there was a lack of effort toward normalizing the LGBT experience (for example, no literature available on this topic or associations with local LGBT groups). Further, aging transgender gay men have especially difficult circumstances in residential facilities because many have the extra concern of keeping up with hormone treatments and dealing with the repercussions of staff seeing them undressed in an environment that is likely transphobic.

Regardless of gender or sexual orientation, most care homes frown upon sexual activity among residents, or even have a total prohibition on sex. Whatever might just be tolerated for cisgender and straight residents around sex, is not very likely to be tolerated in the case of their non-cisgender and gay counterparts.

Gay men with disabilities face similar issues to those gay men who are aging. O'Shea et al. (2020) found that:

> the variety of identities LGBTIQA+ people with disability hold tend to be critically misunderstood in services they rely on, including health services, disability services, LGBTIQA+ services…While some participants felt able to present their 'whole self' in different settings, or found comfort with selective or partial disclosure, many people expressed discomfort, frustration, and despair at having to 'wear a heterosexual, cisgender mask' in disability services, and of feeling excluded from LGBTIQA+ spaces that they could [not] access or that did not recognise their experience of disability.
>
> (p. 8091)

Drexler (2018) points to how "institutions dealing with disability are not properly set up to deal with issues pertaining to the discourse of *disabled sexuality*" (p. 144) and they fail "to recognize the queerness of disabled sexuality", making it "problematic for some people with disabilities to express their sexuality or have sexual relations" (p. 145).

Another intersection of gay men that are especially prone to discrimination and isolation are those who are kinky or practice kink/bondage, discipline/domination, sadism/submission, and masochism (BDSM). For dominants and submissives, society's stigma related to BDSM play often discourages them from accepting and engaging in their desires (Hebert & Weaver, 2015). This stigma will also often cause people within this community to stay closeted around family and friends. Barker, Iantaffi, and Gupta (2007) found that misunderstandings and false assumptions around kink/BDSM are also prevalent among mental health professionals. A lot of therapists believe that someone turns to kink/BDSM only if they have experienced intense mental health issues or sexual trauma in their past. This is simply not true. So for kinksters who happen to be dealing with mental health issues and need guidance on how to connect with others, seeking mental health assistance is often not a safe option and could wind up causing further harm.

Self-Medicating with Substances

How do some gay men choose to deal with all of this shame foisted upon them? A number of gay men self-medicate with substances. McCabe, Bostwick, Hughes, West, and Boyd (2010) show how discrimination around sexual orientation, gender, and race/ethnicity contribute to the high risk of substance use disorders for LGB adults when compared to their heterosexual counterparts. And Caputi, Smith, Strathdee, and Ayers (2018) show that elevated risk of substance use is also present for LGBQ adolescents, "suggesting that this community's exposure to substance use may occur early in the life course" (p. 1033). Many gay men are using these substances to directly medicate themselves to be able to have shame-free sex. However, they are often unaware of how the usage of these substances can ultimately decrease their ability to experience pleasure from life and sex.

References

Barker, M., Iantaffi, A., & Gupta, C. (2007). Kinky clients, kinky counselling? The challenges and potentials of BDSM. In L. Moon (Ed.), *Feeling queer or queer feelings: Radical approaches to counselling sex, sexualities and genders* (106–124). London, UK: Routledge.

Caputi, T.L., Smith, L.R., Strathdee, S.A., & Ayers, J.W. (2018). Substance use among lesbian, gay, bisexual, and questioning adolescents in the United States, 2015. *American Journal of Public Health, 108*(8), 1031–1034.

Drexler, O. (2018). Disability and queerness: Exploration of disability and sexuality in autoethnography and institutional ethnography. *Michigan Sociological Review*, *32*, 133–147.

Greenan, D, & Tunnell, G. (2003). *Couple therapy with gay men*. New York, NY: The Guilford Press.

Hebert, A., & Weaver, A. (2015). Perks, problems, and the people who play: A qualitative exploration of dominant and submissive BDSM roles. *The Canadian Journal of Human Sexuality, 24*(1), 49–62.

Jenkins, D., & Johnson, L.B. (2004). Unethical treatment of gay and lesbian people with 5conversion therapy. *Families in Society, 85*(4), 557–561.

Johnson, S.D., Rostosky, S.S., & Riggle, E.D.B. (2022). In R. Harvey, M.J. Murphy, J.J. Bigner, & J.L. Wetchler (Eds.), *Handbook of LGBTQ-affirmative couple and family therapy*. New York, NY: Routledge.

McCabe, S.E., Bostwick, W.B., Hughes, T.L., West, B.T., & Boyd, C.J. (2010). The relationships between discrimination and substance use disorder among lesbian, gay, and bisexual adults in the United States. *American Journal of Public Health, 100*(10), 1946–1952.

Movement Advancement Project. (2022). Retrieved November 23, 2022 from https://www.lgbtmap.org/equality-maps/conversion_therapy

Nadal, K. (2013). *That's so gay!: Microaggressions and the lesbian, gay, bisexual, and transgender community*. Washington, DC: American Psychological Association.

O'Shea, A, Latham, J.R., McNair, Despott, N, Rose, M., Mountford, R., & Frawley, P. (2020). Experiences of LGBTIQA+ people with disability in healthcare and community services: Towards embracing multiple identities. *International Journal of Environmental Research and Public Health, 17*, 8080–8094.

Odets, W. (2019). *Out of the shadows: Reimagining gay men's lives*. New York, NY: Picador.

Perone, A.K., Ingersoll-Dayton, B., & Watkins-Dukhie, K. (2020). Social isolation loneliness among LGBT older adults: Lessons learned from a pilot friendly caller program. *Clinical Social Work Journal, 48*, 126–139.

Ray, T.N., & Parkhill, M.R. (2021). Heteronormativity, disgust sensitivity, and hostile attitudes toward gay men: Potential mechanisms to maintain social hierarchies. *Sex Roles, 84*, 49–60.

Robbins, K. (2018). *Social cognitive shame theory: Understanding shame and society*. Retrieved from ProQuest LLC. (10846123)

Simpson, P., Almack, K., & Walthery, P. (2018). 'We treat them all the same': the attitudes, knowledge and practices of staff concerning old/er lesbian, gay, bisexual and trans residents in care homes. *Aging & Society, 38*, 869–899.

Tinney, J., Dow, B., Maude, P., Purchase, R., Whyte, C., & Barrett, C. (2015). Mental health issues and discrimination among older LGBTI people. *International Psychogeriatrics, 27*(9), 1411–1416.

Wilkinson, W.W., & Roys, A.C. (2005). The components of sexual orientation, religiosity, and heterosexuals' impressions of gay men and lesbians. *The Journal of Social Psychology 145*(1), 65–83.

Chapter 8

Intimacy Issues

While relationship quality has been shown to be the same or better for same-sex couples as heterosexual couples (Perales & Baxter, 2018), there are unique issues with which gay men in long-term relationships must contend. I will discuss some of those unique issues as well as some that also happen to overlap with heterosexual relationships so that they are also on your radar for assessment and treatment for gay men.

Being Vulnerable with the "Enemy"

The trouble some gay men have with being vulnerable and sharing intimacy with other men, due to childhood bullying around not being masculine enough (Greenan & Tunnell, 2003), may well lead to decreased desire to engage in sex with a partner or partners. These men are continuously wary of engaging in sex because it could easily trigger a shame experience. Imagine the confusion of loving and finding your partner sexually attractive, but wanting to avoid sex because of the uncomfortable feelings with which it is associated (due to childhood trauma). If each of the men in the relationship feel this way, then the issues around sex are magnified even further. And, as discussed in Chapter 4, because of how gay men had been taught they needed to separate emotions from sex, once emotions are strong within a relationship, sex can seem discordant. Many gay adult men feel the unnecessary and depriving need to "protect their partners from the degradation that sex would inflict, and they protect themselves from being seen as sexually emotional beings by the men with whom they live their daily lives" (Odets, 2019, p. 240).

Issues More Common for Gay Male Relationships

Even if one is comfortable having sex with another man, the likelihood of increased mental health issues for gay men (due to minority discrimination) means increased likelihood of mental health issues playing a role when it

DOI: 10.4324/9781003386322-9

comes to sex. We already saw how anxiety, depression, and body issues get in the way of wanting sex or having pleasurable sex, increasingly so for gay men of color and transgender, and gender non-conforming, disabled, and aging gay men. In addition to mental health, some emotionally charged issues specific to gay men in relationships (versus most heterosexual men) that could get in the way of desire and sex include not all partners being out (or out to the same extent), there being discordance around HIV status, external romantic and sexual relationships, cross-generational relationships, and toxic masculinity.

Gay male relationships may have partners that are out to different degrees. One partner, for example, could be completely out to their family, friends, and co-workers, allowing his partner(s) to join him at all events and be seen as a partner, whereas the other partner could not be out in as many spaces or even not out of the closet at all. This can cause resentment from those partners who are further out of the closet because they tend be more excluded from that partner's life and/or they may feel that since they were brave enough to come out, their partner should as well. This can lead to pressure being put on the more reticent partner who is not as out and feelings of isolation for all partners involved – further decreasing desire for sex within that relationship.

In a relationship that is serodiscordant (where at least one partner has HIV and another does not), there will often be a stigma felt by the person who is HIV+. Even with a loving partner or loving partners, it can be difficult for the HIV+ partner not to take in the untrue and negative messaging that society puts out into the world with regard to what their HIV status says about them as a person and (even on medication and with an undetectable viral load) not feel as if they are putting their partner(s) at a disadvantage or exposing them to a high risk of getting HIV. This could lead to the partner with HIV staying away from sex altogether or from sexual activities that could provide considerable pleasure.

With about 40% of gay men likely in sexually open/non-monogamous relationships (LaSala, 2004), as clinicians, we must be ready to work with the added stressors that come along with multiple partners. While more partners could definitely equate to more loving and stimulation, it will also, naturally, equate to more management of emotions and the need for extremely effective communication skills. And, even when partners have great emotional regulation and communication skills, clinicians must also need to be ready to deal with new relationship energy. Because the chemicals that are present in the body during a new relationship can cause someone to behave differently than they would typically, when a partner enters a new relationship this can do a lot to dysregulate each partner and possibly take time and intimacy away from other partner(s).

"More gay men are open to older partners than straight men. In spite of the gay culture's emphasis on youth, gay men are less subject to traditional societal pressures on males to have a younger spouse" (Kaufman & Phua, 2003, p. 232). This may be because gay men are less beholden to gender stereotypes of heterosexual relationships and/or fertility is not a relevant concern (Kaufman & Phua, 2003). With the higher likelihood of cross-generational relationships among gay men, you also get an increased chance of incompatible sex drives, incongruent abilities to perform certain sex acts, and a lack of connection from being in different life stages.

Wade and Donis (2007) showed that "traditional masculinity ideology was related to lower relationship quality for both gay and heterosexual men" (p. 783). Knowing how much toxic masculinity runs rampant for gay men and that in gay male relationships you will have at least two gay men, the chances of traditional masculinity ideology getting in the way of the relationship and sex is magnified. There can be a lot of shame, defensiveness, and resentment around who winds up playing the roles that are more commonly seen as feminine – from vacuuming to bottoming during sex. Gay Latin men from particular cultures can be especially susceptible to these feelings because they tend to be brought up in a culture that emphasizes masculinity or "machismo". For example, in one study, non-Mexican Latino men had a significantly higher rate (versus white and Black gay men) of only wanting to top when it came to anal sex (Jeffries IV, 2007). Shame, defensiveness, and resentment are not emotions that tend to encourage us to be intimate.

> I will add here a practical aspect of gay male relationships that can serve as an obstacle to having sex as much as partners would like. If the partners want to have anal sex, often the person who is bottoming must "get ready", which means making sure their rectum is free of feces. Most gay men will try to make this happen by douching right before sex and being careful about what they eat on a daily basis. And any issues that could get in the way of being "ready" for a particular sexual encounter (for example, having an upset stomach) could eliminate any intimacy at all, especially if the partners simply equate sex with penetration.

Universal Relationship Issues

Among the relationship issues that are not exclusive to gay men are libido discordance, ineffective communication, unrealistic expectations around what sex should be/look like (especially in a long-term relationship), feeling a need to separate love from lust, and parenting.

References

Greenan, D, & Tunnell, G. (2003). *Couple therapy with gay men*. New York, NY: The Guilford Press.

Jeffries IV, W.L. (2007). A comparative analysis of homosexual behaviors, sex role preferences, and anal sex proclivities in Latino and non-Latino Men. *Archives of Sexual Behavior 38*, 765–778.

Kaufman, G., & Phua, V.C. (2003). Is ageism alive in date selection among men? Age requests among gay and straight men in internet personal ads. *Journal of Men's Studies 11*(2), 225–236.

LaSala, M.C. (2004). Extradyadic sex and gay male couples: Comparing monogamous and nonmonogamous relationships. *Families in Society 85*(3), 405–412.

Odets, W. (2019). *Out of the shadows: Reimagining gay men's lives*. New York, NY: Picador.

Perales, F., & Baxter, J. (2018). Sexual identity and relationships quality in Australia and the United Kingdom. *Interdisciplinary Journal of Applied Family Science 67*, 55–69.

Wade, J.C., & Donis, E. (2007). Masculinity ideology, male Identity, and romantic relationship quality among heterosexual and gay men. *Sex Roles 57*, 775–786.

Chapter 9

Hookup Apps

The Apps Keep Drawing You Back

Ding! Ding! "I won – someone "woofed" at me." Ding! Ding! "I won – someone sent me a message." Ding! Ding! "I won - nine more guys clicked on my profile." Ding! Ding! "I won – I have worth." Most social media, dating, and hookup apps are no different from slot machines in terms of them being set up to keep us coming back, with the hope that this time we will finally get what we want. The jackpot with the hookup apps is a very fleeting sense of external validation. So fleeting, that one often goes back for more. And, like slots, more times than not, the "player" winds up losing. This is particularly the case when they look to the hookup apps to find a long-term romantic partner, but it even applies when they are looking to just hook up. It is not uncommon to talk to a guy for a while about getting together to hook up and for the other person not to follow through. I believe this happens because a lot of men are on there just to try to fulfill some need or desire through texting, with no intention and/or capability to meet up and there are others with the desire to meet, but who find that following through proves too anxiety-provoking for them. Whether looking for a long-term partner or sex, men often wind up having spent way more time than they wanted on these apps. While hookup apps have the potential of being a tool for eventually finding great sex, I will share some of the downsides of these apps that lead gay men to have further issues with sex.

Increasing the Feelings of Shame and Isolation

There is very little that is not allowed on the profiles of hookup apps, so these platforms are full of landmines that explode, with the casualty being an increase in shame. "No Fats, Femmes, or Asians" is a popular phrase/request included in profiles. Another common term in profiles that shames femininity in gay men is "masc4masc". This means that the person posting this message considers themselves masculine and that they do not want to connect

DOI: 10.4324/9781003386322-10

with anyone who does not also look and behave in a "masculine" way. There are numerous profiles without any pictures, perpetuating the idea that it is shameful to be known as gay or as a man looking to have sex with other men. Profiles will refer to only wanting to connect with people who do not have HIV, often using the term "clean" to describe them, and implying that one is "dirty" if they have HIV. A typical chat exchange is someone reaching out with a "hi", seeing that the intended receiver has looked at the text and their profile, and then decided to not respond at all – leaving the person who reached out to feel as if they were not even worthy of a response. And ghosting is ever-present, even after chatting with someone for weeks and planning to meet up or having met up. Good luck feeling good enough about yourself to have sex when using hookup apps.

These apps also help to keep gay men isolated. Odets (2019) highlights how hookup apps objectify men and give them an unfulfilling pretence of connecting with other human beings:

> …it encourages physical interaction with "things" to the exclusion of intellectual and emotional intimacy…While, as adults, many with fulfilled lives use the apps largely for recreational hookups, a majority of men use them to address isolation and a lack of intimacy. They are looking for *something*, something substantial and important: but for every connection that truly grows into something meaningful, thousands are merely objectifying, and thus disappointing.
>
> (pp. 162–163)

Philip Zimbardo's famous experiment of a simulated prison environment showed us how, when people's faces and names are hidden, they naturally will be more aggressive toward others. This reality is alive and well on the hookup apps. As mentioned, numerous profiles do not have their pictures; when they do, they are not always of the person's face. Even when face pics are shared, there is still a sense of anonymity because hookup apps allow the user to use whatever profile name they wish. Often profile names are an indication of what they are looking for around sex, not any derivation of someone's real name. Combine this lack of feeling a sense of kindness toward strangers with a lot of men who are already feeling unacceptable (looking to reject others in order to attempt to vindicate themselves) (Odets, 2019) and you have a powder keg of inappropriate treatment. So, where a gay man goes to look for sex could easily wind up being where he gets abused and further shamed.

Profiles Share Access to Drugs

The hookup apps are also known as places where someone can easily find out where to access illegal drugs. The most common drug is crystal methamphetamine, often referred to as "tina". On profiles, to advertise that there is a place to have sex where there will also be crystal meth, "T"s used in the middle of words will be purposely capitalized. In addition, the terms "party" or "party and play" in a profile mean that sex and drugs (often crystal meth) will be happening with that app user or at a certain location. As mentioned in Chapter 1, some gay men are drawn to chem sex as a way to temporarily rid themselves of the shame they have around sex, paying a heavy price of recovery after using. But even while using, there may also be a heavy price to pay. When a person is on crystal meth, their decision-making skills are severely compromised, easily straying from taking care of themselves the way they would if they were not intoxicated. They can more easily be persuaded to take more of the drug or other drugs, as well as becoming victims of sexual abuse. Some of my clients have intended to party and play for a night, only to find themselves wound up being awake, having sex, and being high for days, without any clear idea of what happened to them during that time. Studies do show that those using the hookup apps do have higher levels of sexual risk and drug use (Gibson, Kramer, & Bryan, 2022; Pravosud, Ballard, Holloway, & Young, 2022). Combining the allure of shame-free sex with a platform that intensifies shame and makes it obvious where to indulge in chem sex can be a recipe for disaster.

A Worse Space for Intersectionality

Not surprisingly, hookup apps also offer another space for Black men to be discriminated against. Wade and Pear (2022) found that young sexual minority Black men experienced rejection due to being Black and that they saw whiteness as a preferred characteristic when using Grindr. Equally, when Black men are sought after on these apps, it is often the expectation that they will have a big black cock (BBC) and they will need to be able to show this to be the case before meeting up. And even hookup apps created specifically for the gay male Black community are not a panacea, because they are still hookup apps – full of the trappings these platforms tend to create and encourage to flourish.

Hookup apps can also be an especially confusing space for those within the transgender and non-binary communities. Masullo and Coppola (2021) looked into transgender and non-binary individuals and dating apps (which also included hookup apps) and found that, "On the one hand, they are places of emancipation; on the other, they perpetuate the exclusion mechanisms experienced offline" (p. 338) and the genderist models mostly present in these apps cause conflict for non-binary and transgender individuals. Their study also shows that "it is not uncommon to run into discriminatory phenomena (e.g. online shaming) by transphobic people" (p. 336) or people who do not accept or recognize minority genders. And, while there are some hookup apps specifically for transgender, non-binary, and/or queer (TGNBQ) communities, the larger ones are not gay-specific, so can prove quite challenging for gay TGNBQ men.

For persons with disabilities and/or chronic illness some hookup apps can offer an easier time of looking for someone to have sex with because accommodations needed around sex can be detailed before meeting and the user knows ahead of time how far they will have to travel to meet. However, they can also be a place of further discrimination. "The stigmatization or stratification of desirability in the gay community is rather covert. White, able-bodied, cisgender, 'straight-acting' males are the desirable normate at the top of the hierarchy" (Cheslik & Wright, 2021, p. 1034). "Queer spaces…as a general rule are not inclusive of disabled and 'other' bodies" (Cheslik & Wright, 2021, p. 1035). This definitely transfers to the digital space of hookup apps, where those who are disabled and/or chronically ill have reported being rejected or fetishized/objectified because of their disability or illness (Cheslik & Wright, 2021). Cheslik and Wright (2021) compare the difficulty of these individuals testing the waters on hookup apps on how others will receive them as they reveal their disability and/or illness to those who worry about rejection around revealing if they have HIV. For persons with disabilities and/or chronic illness, the hookup apps can be extra cruel waters to navigate.

References

Cheslik, B., & Wright, S.J. (2021). The impact of gay social networking applications on dating in the Deaf gay community. *Sexuality & Culture 25*, 1025–1040.

Gibson, L.P., Kramer, E.B., & Bryan, A.D. (2022). Geosocial networking app use associated with sexual risk behavior and pre-exposure prophylaxis use among gay, bisexual, and other men who have sex with men: Cross-sectional web-based survey. *JMIR Formative Research 6*(6), e35548.

Masullo, M. & Coppola, M. (2021). Scripts and sexual markets of transgender people on online dating apps: A netnographic study. *Italian Sociological Review 11*(4S), 319–341.

Odets, W. (2019). *Out of the shadows: Reimagining gay men's lives*. New York, NY: Picador.

Pravosud, V., Ballard, A.M., Holloway, I.W., & Young, A.M. (2022). Online partner seeking and sexual behaviors among men who have sex with men from small and midsized towns: Cross-sectional study. *JMIR Formative Research 6*(6), e35056.

Wade, R.M., & Pear, M.M. (2022). A good app Is hard to find: Examining differences in racialized sexual discrimination across online intimate partner-seeking venues. *International Journal of Environmental Research and Public Health 19*, 8727–8741.

Chapter 10

Sexuality Assessment

Conversations to Have with Gay Men

Covering assessment is our transition into treatment, as assessment is constantly occurring throughout the therapeutic process and is a useful tool for interventions. When I begin to explore with my clients their sexual histories and current narratives, I ask that they first be as present as they are able. We start with a quick mindfulness exercise of each of us paying attention to our breath (not changing our breath, just paying attention to it) and feeling our feet on the floor (for a sense of being grounded). I let them know that they do not have to answer anything that makes them uncomfortable. This helps the client feel safe and in control and I make mental notes of what they are uncomfortable talking about, so that I am careful with those topics in the future. And, finally, I let them know that this will be a conversation, with me exploring, but not asking a barrage of questions.

Throughout the assessment and my work with clients, I am very careful about the language that I use. I do not want to further shame or create anxiety for a client by referring to a sexual issue they are having as a "dysfunction". I want to reiterate that just because a part of our body is not working the way we would like it to, or the way in which the media says it should, does not mean that it is broken in any way.

I like to start from the beginning, as it gives me an informed foundation to better understand what is currently going on in their lives around sex. When looking into a client's sexual history I use Iasenza's (2020) approach of beginning with the question: "What is your earliest memory of sexuality?" (p. 48) and then I slowly explore what that experience meant for them, and what narratives came from that experience that they still believe, and also to specifically look for any boundary transgressions or relational or attachment wounds that may have come from that experience.

I also want to explore how they learned about sexuality throughout childhood, adolescence, and young adulthood. I want to get a sense of what messaging they received around sexuality, from where, and how those messages

DOI: 10.4324/9781003386322-11

effected their sense of themselves as sexual beings. We also discuss what they heard specifically about gay men and sex. Often, I wind up exploring:

- How intersectionality contributed to their sexual narrative, typically ethnicity/race, ability, gender, weight, and socio-economic and immigration status.
- What it meant for them to hide their attraction and feelings in order to survive and stay connected to family and peers.
- What it was like to long for the touch of another male, but not be able to get that as easily as their straight peers.
- If they felt dirty for having to keep their sexual and romantic relationships secret in order to not be ostracized.
- What it meant for their sexual identity if family members made overt negative comments or microaggressions about gay men, relationships, and sex.
- What it meant for their sexual identity if their religion was telling them that what they wanted to do was unnatural and a sin.
- For those growing up in the 1980s, what it was like to have sex so explicitly linked to pain, disability, isolation, neglect, and death.

I also want to explore items around their current sexual lives. Below are questions I tend to weave into conversations.

- What do they look to get out of sex? Metz and McCarthy (2012) advance five basic purposes for sex, four of which I have seen to be applicable to gay men: pleasure, intimacy, stress reduction, and self-esteem. I do get a bit concerned when I hear a client speak to self-esteem as the motivator, knowing how much shame gay men are living with. And when my clients speak of getting an improved sense of self-esteem through sex, it typically means that they focus on performance and getting specific feedback from the partner or partners to let them know they are "doing sex well/right". While validating the common desire to increase their self-esteem through sex, I also make sure they are aware of the dangers of doing so.
- What parts of their body are erogenous zones? I encourage them to think beyond the penis, anus, and nipples. I casually ask about the possibilities of other body parts, like the elbow, the ear, and the back of the knee. This helps expand opportunity for pleasure and takes the pressure off stimulating just the same body parts each time and expecting those body parts to always perform in a certain way. This also helps take focus away from genitalia if this is not where the client wants to focus.
- What kinds of sex, sex scenes, or sex roles stimulate them? Here we talk about what kind of sex they are into, what they would like to try, experiences with or desires surrounding kink/bondage, discipline/domination,

sadism/submission, and masochism (BDSM), how important power dynamics are during sex, and how safer-sex practices fit into what turns them on.

- What is masturbation like for them? I often find that gay men are quickly yanking at their cocks just to have some release. If this is the case, we talk about the benefits of intentional self-pleasure when masturbating, making use of their entire body, and toys or household items they can safely use on all parts of their body.
- What negative experiences or difficulties are they currently having related to sex? I like to ask this as given, in order to normalize that we all have issues with sex. This decreases shame and increases the likelihood that they will share what they are having issues around. I would follow this up with my typical medical intake questions (please see Chapter 11).
- What are they currently enjoying about sex? I like to bring the discussion back to strengths and what is going right for them around sex. Here we talk about what is actually occurring for them around sex – frequency, quality, how they are dealing with shame around sex between men, if power dynamics are being played out during sex, how they are dealing with being vulnerable with other men, and what are they are practicing in terms of safer sex.
- For my transgender and non-binary clients, I add in a few questions from Fielding's (2021) book, *Trans Sex*.

  - "Who are your erotic models?", "What in your life makes you feel liberated?", and "What does your most pleasurable life look like?" (p. 135)
  - What do they call their genitals?

- What has changed around sex as they have aged? Again, I like to normalize that sex becomes different with age. A lot of our sexual identity was decided when we were young and had young bodies (Klein, 2012). I want to make sure my clients realize that while sex is different as they age, it can be even better because of how much over time they have learned about their bodies and what brings them pleasure.
- Which sense is most important to them during sex? They may have never realized how much their senses can cause them to be turned on or off. An awareness of this could allow greater stimulation during sex and the avoidance of anything that may get in the way of enjoying sex or being present. For example, if they realize that for them smell is actually the scent that is most connected to being turned on or off, then we make sure they are positively enhancing smell for themselves during sex.
- What adaptations have they already tried to increase their sexual pleasure? Here we tend to talk about toys, lube, and any devices that tend to increase accessibility for those who are disabled.

When exploring a sexual assessment with couples, I see the clients individually, as I prefer for them to feel free to share all issues with me, including those they may hold back from saying in front of their partner(s) due to concern of insulting them or hurting their feelings.

I use Peixoto's (2022) suggestions for sex therapy assessment of gay male couples and explore the following:

- "…gender role socialization, preferred sexual scripts, and sexual role models" (p. 129).
- The role power plays in the relationship, including how each member of the relationships feels decisions get made, who tends to make the decisions, if one of them feels they are carrying more of the emotional labor burden, differences in socio-economic, cultural, and educational backgrounds, and current professions.
- External factors that may be getting in the way of sex, like work and extended family stress and mental health issues.
- What has already been tried to deal with their sexual issues.

I also typically ask questions around how out of the closet each of them is and, if there is a large difference, how those feelings may play a role in distancing them from one another. I also explore if HIV and difficulties of being vulnerable with another man create distance.

Knowing someone's fantasies can provide a plethora of useful information that we may not be able to get otherwise. "Since sexual fantasies are created in order to temporarily master nonsexual conflicts involving guilt, worry, shame, and helplessness, understanding their meaning can help us shine a light into the deepest corners of who we are" (Bader, 2002, p. 280). When exploring their fantasies, I find that Morin's (1995) guidance works well for gay men:

- Pretending that they are having trouble being aroused, then describing, based on what they know about their own sexuality, a fantasy that would have the best chance of arousing them.
- Exploring what about this fantasy arouses them.
- Giving detail about the most intense part of this fantasy.
- Paying special attention to memorable details of these fantasies, which tend to be:
  - First experiences of something or a surprise in the narrative (for example, falling in love with your best friend)
  - Something special or distinct about the situation or partner(s) (for example, a hot stranger that will never be seen again)
  - Attention paid to timing (for example, a weekend of love making)

I use this information to help the client better understand what they may be looking for from sex (for example, playing a submissive role as a way to escape from an over-demanding career or loud sex to combat the shame of having sex with another man) and what might give them maximum pleasure.

References

Bader, M.J. (2002). *Arousal: The secret logic of sexual fantasies*. New York, NY: St. Martin's Press.

Fielding, L. (2021). *Trans sex*. New York, NY: Routledge.

Iasenza, S. (2020). *Transforming sexual narratives: A relational approach to sex therapy*. New York, NY: Routledge.

Klein, M. (2012). Sexual intelligence: What we really want from sex and how to get it. New York, NY: HarperCollins.

Metz, M.E., & McCarthy, B.W. (2012). The good enough sex (GES) model: Perspective and clinical applications. In P.J. Kleinplatz (Ed.), *New directions in sex therapy*. New York, NY: Routledge.

Morin, J. (1995). *The erotic mind*. New York, NY: HarperCollins Publishers.

Peixoto, M.M. (2022). Affirming diversity and targeting pleasure: Sex therapy for gay male couples. In R. Harvey, M.J. Murphy, J.J. Bigner, & J.L. Wetchler (Eds.), *Handbook of LGBTQ-Affirmative couple and family therapy*. New York, NY: Routledge.

Chapter 11

Medical and Physiological Interventions

Getting the Right Doctors

As previously mentioned, the medical field does not tend to be sex-positive. These professionals possess the same ideas as American society at large, that sex is a taboo subject, and they have not likely been educated on how to talk about and deal with sexual issues. That makes our jobs as therapists even more important, as we need to try to curate a list of local medical professionals that are actually going to be able to help our clients with their sexual issues. A lot of this will be through word of mouth – learning from clients or other professionals – or from making visits with local medical offices. You want to get a sense if these professionals have clients that are gay men and how they handle these clients bringing up issues with erection, desire, anal sex, and ejaculation. You will typically know quickly from your initial interactions with them if they have had experience of such matters and what is their level of comfort.

Other options are searchable directories on www.polyfriendly.org, www.kapprofessionals.org, and www.optionsforsexualhealth.org (in Canada), Planned Parenthood, and lists already put together by local kink/bondage, discipline/domination, sadism/submission, and masochism (BDSM), consensually non-monogamous, and other sex-positive groups.

If you are not already, please make yourself familiar with pelvic floor specialists. They are able to treat issues with orgasm, ejaculation, and pain during sex. Again, you want to find one that will be a good fit for your client. In addition to the questions I suggested above to see if the doctor is sex-affirming, you may want to see if a pelvic floor specialist you are looking to refer will assess whether or not the client will be ready for a pelvic exam on the first visit. Those who just automatically give clients a pelvic exam on their first visit are likely not going to truly consider where your client is and what are their needs. A great resource for men and pelvic and sexual health is drsusieg.com.

DOI: 10.4324/9781003386322-12

Prepping for Doctor Visits

Even if you do find a sex-affirming doctor in your community that works with gay men, you still will have other hurdles to overcome. For example, costs (whether or not the client has insurance) and how that doctor deals with your client's intersectionality – so do they have expertise and/or comfort with working with the transgender, non-binary, aging, disabled, consensually non-monogamous, kink/BDSM, fat, and/or diverse race and ethnicity communities? Most gay male clients looking to deal with sexual issues are going to have to settle. Let us as therapists be aware of this and work with our clients to best prepare for them for these visits.

White coat syndrome is a reality for many of us – we get nervous at doctor appointments. Combine that baseline with having to talk about sex with a stranger who may (or may not) be able to treat or accept you as a whole person. We need our clients to have self-compassion and confidence when going into these appointments and I typically suggest bringing in notes about what they would like to discuss, taking notes during the session, doing some mindfulness exercises before and after the session, and setting up some self-care for after the session (perhaps having a close friend available for a call). I also work with some reality testing around doctors being human beings (not all-knowing gods) who may not have all the answers and who also have the ability to be just as narrow-minded as anyone else.

Medication Transparency

You will also look to doctors to weigh in on whether the client's current medications, or ones that will be prescribed, have sexual side effects. As mentioned in Chapter 3, serotonin contributes to less desire to have sex, so selective serotonin reuptake inhibitors (SSRIs), typically given for depression and anxiety, can lead to issues in these areas. By contrast, Wellbutrin is a common option for depression that works with norepinephrine (not serotonin), so it tends to be less intrusive when it comes to sex. Other medications for depression that are less likely to interfere with sex are Remeron, Nefazodone, Trintellix, and Viibryd – but, of course, they do have other side effects. Mood stabilizers Lithium and Depakote do not tend to have a negative impact on sex. Compared to most atypical anti-psychotics, Abilify and Seroquel may be the preferred options in order to attempt to have less of an effect on sex. Adding Buspar to an anti-anxiety regimen may help reduce sexual side effects, and adding Wellbutrin may do the same for someone that needs to take an SSRI.

In addition to asking a doctor if medications should be switched or added, your client may also want to ask their doctor if any of the following might help them avoid sexual issues related to their current medication regimen: a dosage reduction, skipping a dose, drug holidays, and changing the time of day medication is taken.

Arousal and Erection

A common medical go-to for men with sexual issues is to figure out if testosterone is "too low". I have heard mixed opinions as to whether or not adjusting testosterone actually helps, especially considering that one man could have "low" testosterone levels and not have any issues around sex – as levels vary from individual to individual. However, if your client is going down this route, you want to make sure that their testosterone levels are measured twice, at the same time of day as the first test. Among the methods to increase testosterone naturally are exercise (especially cardio), sleeping well, and having balanced diet.

Another medical go-to for men is taking a pill to help with erection issues: these include Viagra, Cialis, Levitra, or Stendra. It is important for those who take these medications to know that they will not magically make the person have an erection. The person will have to be thinking or experiencing something arousing so that the brain sends a message down the spinal cord to allow the penis to fill with blood. Because these pills increase blood flow, taking them while also using or taking nitrates (like poppers – commonly used by gay men for sex) and/or blood pressure medications can produce significantly and dangerously low blood pressure and while taking or using alpha blockers, alcohol, or grapefruit juice can contribute to low blood pressure.

Treating Ejaculation Issues

If your client is having trouble with orgasm or ejaculation, you will want to have a doctor look into hypo or hyperthyroidism as a possible cause. Also, if your client is above the age of 50 and is not getting erections at all, even when masturbating or upon waking up, you will want a doctor to look into the potential of plaque building up.

If your client is ejaculating sooner than they would like, has already seen a doctor about this, and you already challenged false messaging around there being some universal amount of time someone is supposed to have sex before ejaculating, there are interventions that you can instruct your client on to try at home. These are the squeeze and start-and-start methods and desensitizers.

With the squeeze method, at home, when your client gets close to ejaculating, they squeeze the end of their penis where the head meets the shaft. After squeezing for several seconds, the urge to ejaculate will likely subside.

Trying this numerous times should help delay ejaculation during that particular time and practicing often may help the client no longer need the method to delay ejaculation.

For the start-and-stop technique you first want to establish with your client their arousal scale, from 1 through 10, with 9 being right before they ejaculate and 10 being have ejaculated. Then, at home, they are to masturbate to about a 6, stop, go back to 3, back to 6, stop, go up to 3, back to 6, down to 3, and then all the way up to 10. In this chapter, Worksheet 1 (also available on this book's product page at www.routledge.com/9781032478715) will help your clients with this exercise. Practicing this method allows the client to work the muscles needed to gain greater control of their ejaculation.

Desensitizers are a quicker and external way to deal with ejaculation issues. They will provide a numbing effect so that the user is not as sensitive to the friction on their penis. This means, of course, that the user will not feel as much sensation as they would typically and, with most desensitizers, this will also numb all parts of the partner(s) that the product gets on. Please be aware that those who use desensitizers for anal sex run the risk of the person topping and bottoming not feeling the pain that would be an indication of tearing or bleeding, which means plenty of pain later and increasing the risk of sexually transmitted infections. Numbing agents are also available inside some condoms and just using most condoms (even without a numbing agent) could decrease penis sensitivity.

Treating Pain While Bottoming

Another physiological area that some gay men may want to explore is experiencing pain while bottoming (anodyspareunia). If they have already ruled out a medical issue, here are some non-psychological interventions that may help.

Be intentional around lubricant (lube) usage. The U.S. Food and Drug Administration (FDA) does not oversee the production of lube, so clients will want to be especially careful of what they are putting in and on their bodies. Some of the chemicals used in certain lubes can cause a painful reaction. If an ingredient in the lube is not what is causing you pain, then you want to make sure you are using enough of the right kind of lube. Lubes come in various consistencies and for bottoming one with a denser consistency or thicker viscosity will be especially good to avoid any friction that may cause pain. And when choosing between water and silicone-based lube, always remember that silicone lube is not safe to use with most condoms and silicone toys.

Now let's get acquainted with the anus. It allows feces to be eliminated from the body. To accomplish this, the interior and exterior sphincters (which are circular muscles) ease up on constriction to allow the feces to leave the body. While we have some control over the extent of constriction of our external sphincter, this is not the case for our internal sphincter, which lives underneath the exterior sphincter. A tight sphincter tends to lead to pain. But all is not lost. Like other involuntary muscles, the best way to get the internal sphincter to relax is through deep breathing. The deep breathing I tend to recommend is breathing in for a three count and then out slowly, like breathing out through a straw, for a four or five count. The client should then work on increasing each of the counts when ready, as long as the exhale is always a longer count than the inhale.

If your client has the financial means and safe access to and storage of sex toys, they may also want to use toys to help get their anus muscles become accustomed to having an object enter it. Butt plugs are a good place to start. They will want to make sure that their toys are made out of safe materials. For most sex toys, silicon, hard plastic, and glass are the best materials, as they prevent bacteria from seeping into them (which happens with porous materials like rubber and jelly). They will also want to be careful about Phthalates, which are a chemical rubber softener that has been classified by the FDA as a probable carcinogen. To maintain toys, they will want to use a soap (that is *not* anti-bacterial) to clean them and store them in places that will help them to avoid dust and dirt. They will also want to make sure that any toy being used in the anus has a bottom that will keep it from slipping fully into their butt. This is typically a flared bottom. Further, in most cases, they will want an anus toy that is tapered (so the initial part going in is smaller and allows the sphincter to gradually work its way up to more girth). Butt plugs come in different sizes, so beginners should start with smaller butt plugs and then work their way to larger ones. And when using these, they will also want to make sure they are using plenty of lube that works for their body and anal play, but, again, not silicone lube with silicone toys (as they will cause the silicone to degrade over time, making the toy less comfortable and more porous). Another possible tool is the hand. If your client is able, they can look to use a rubber glove (to avoid scratching) and lube, start with inserting their smallest finger, and then working their way up to larger and/or more fingers from there.

Worksheet 1: Start-and-Stop Technique to Delay Ejaculation

There is no standard amount of time every single person should be waiting until ejaculation. Ejaculation time differs for us all and you likely have a very inflated number in your head for the amount of time someone takes before ejaculating. However, if you are interested in delaying your ejaculation, you can try the start-and-stop technique.

Use the steps below over time to help you work the muscles needed to gain greater control of your ejaculation.

1 Use the below 10-point scale, where a 9 is when you are just about to ejaculate.
2 Masturbate to a 6 on the scale.
3 Once you reach a 6, go back to 3.
4 Once you get back to 3, go back to 6.
5 Repeat steps 3 and 4 another two times.
6 The next time you go down to 3, go up to 10 (ejaculate).

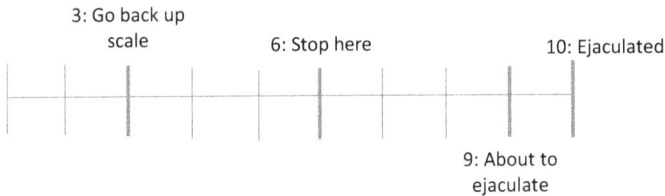

Chapter 12

Healing Developmental Issues and Improving Sexual Experiences

Narrative Therapy to Heal Developmental Trauma

I have found the collaborative nature of Narrative Therapy to be a great clinical tool when helping someone explore perceptions of themselves that were created during a childhood of being a victim of systemic discrimination. Because these perceptions of self are so hard-wired, and reinforced daily, getting the client to challenge the scripts they have already written for themselves can be very difficult. Getting to truths on their own, through their own stories and not through skills or insights I share as a therapist, tends to be very effective at re-wiring their brain.

The tenets of Narrative Therapy that I have found especially effective when working on the developmental stories of gay men are:

- Externalization: When telling their story, being able to see how they are not the problem but instead that the problem is separate from them. This externalization can be key in getting gay men to not be mired in shame, but instead focus on healing themselves from the true culprits – typically, the systems that surround them.
- Deconstruction: To help them see their initial stories more realistically, we go into the details of their narrative, helping them to steer clear of the vague notions that easily lead to self-blame. When they look deeper, they are able to see that they have internalized a hate that is unfairly emanating from the outside world.
- Unique Outcomes: This rewriting of their story allows them to learn more about their true identity, see themselves as beings who do not need to carry shame, and see how much value they add to world.

Case Study

Fred is a 37-year-old, white, abled-bodied, gay, cisgender male, who uses he/him pronouns. He grew up in the Midwest with politically conservative

DOI: 10.4324/9781003386322-13

parents who were very religious. While some of his siblings were not conservative, they were all very devout to their religion. This religion allowed its followers to accept those who were gay; however, it was considered a sin for them to "act on" being gay. From an early age Fred knew that he was different in a way that was considered bad and he could never make good. This was confirmed for him when, at the age of 7, he was in the room he shared with one of his brothers and started singing along to music while using a stuffed animal as his singing partner. His brother then immediately called him a "fag" before proceeding to beat him up. That same night, at the dinner table, this brother announced Fred's behavior to the rest of the family. His sisters and mother were quiet and looked crestfallen, and his father and brothers teased him about it. He felt doomed for a life of hiding who he was simply to stay alive and retain some connection to his family. To stay safe from his family, he often isolated himself, which led to eventual teasing from the family for being a "weirdo loner." The messaging from his family was echoing what he heard at school from his peers.

When Fred was 17, he thought he might find support from the brother who was closest in age to him if he were to come out, so he told this brother. Upon hearing what Fred had to say, this brother proceeded to beat him up and tell him that he could not tell his father because the father would kill Fred. At the age of 19, in his dresser drawer, Fred's mother found a letter he had received from a guy with whom he was having sex. She confronted him with it, telling him he was disgusting, and then never mentioned the letter or what she now knew about her son again. At that point, he stopped having sex with anyone.

As a young adult, Fred moved out on his own and tried to live a more authentic life, without the watchful and judgmental eyes of his family. However, while he knew that for him sex was an important aspect of living his authentic life, he could not bring himself to have sex with men. He knew he was aroused by men, and that he wanted to have sex with men; however, he was having trouble getting erect when having sex with men and would leave those sexual encounters full of shame, sadness, and anger for not being able to perform. Over time, he decided to exclusively bottom. While he was able to experience some physical pleasure from bottoming, he still left those encounters with a lot of shame.

Clinical Impressions

Fred grew up in a hostile environment. The place where he was supposed to feel safe, secure, and loved unconditionally was filled with land mines that could explode at any second if he moved, talked, or looked in any way that spoke to his being gay. His childhood brain told him that the treatment he was receiving must be his fault because it would be too devasting for his chances of survival in life if his parents were actually to blame and therefore unable to ultimately be his protectors. This irrational thinking, in order to prevent his world from falling into chaos, became hard-wiring that stayed with him into adulthood. I was also thinking that this idea of him being to blame was further emphasized for him by his religion, peers, and community speaking of being gay as evil. And since society sees being gay as just about men having sex with men, it made sense that when Fred would have sex with men, he would be reminded of the false belief that he was this bad thing that nobody wanted around, and that, therefore, he was having issues with erection and sex with men.

I was feeling sadness and anger as Fred shared a story I have heard countless times from my clients and of which I had lived my own version. I also felt anger toward organized religion. I was heartbroken when Fred shared that his mother referred to him as disgusting. Yet I was also happy. I was happy that Fred wanted more from his sexual experiences and was seeking guidance for this.

Treatment

After our assessment, we first discussed Fred seeing his primary care physician to explore any possible medical issues around his erection. Then, after a lot of validation and teaching of self-compassion for what childhood Fred went through and what adult Fred was currently going through, we began to rewrite his narrative. We began by using Fred's adult brain and body to revisit a situation that childhood Fred experienced that he remembered feeling shame around. I asked that he choose a situation that he felt safe sharing and would let me know if that memory became too triggering for him, keeping an eye on his heart rate throughout the telling of the narrative. This is when he shared the story about singing out loud with the stuffed animal and the repercussions of that behavior. I slowed down the story and asked Fred to think about whether or not that carefree, fun-loving, childhood Fred behavior was "actually" wrong or bad or inappropriate in any way? He thought about this and was able to share how he was just being a kid and was not looking to hurt anyone. When we explored why his family may have acted the way they did if childhood Fred was not trying to hurt anyone, he was able to consider that each family member had their own insecurities around seeing his behavior – contributing to their own violent behavior or neglect. He was able to see how society was not only sending him messaging that being gay was bad, but was also sending this messaging to his family. I confirmed this assertion and also provided some insight into how misogyny (in addition to homophobia) could have also been why he, as a boy with more societally defined feminine behaviors than most boys, was a target. Fred became open to the possibility that, like most males, his brothers and fathers could have had their own insecurities around feminine aspects of themselves (because that is naively seen as showing weakness or being less of man) and seeing these feminine aspects in Fred could have caused a strong acting-out response from his brothers and his father. We also explored how religion can be of great value but also how its strong messaging of right and wrong and its being interpreted by (mostly) men with their own fears and biases lead it to put out messaging that is incorrect and harmful – or, at the very least, open to other interpretations.

Fred was able to see how so much of what he was thinking and feeling about himself was not factual and actually came from scared and uninformed people. We explored how anyone would have extreme difficulty not taking in and believing this faulty messaging, as it surrounds and penetrates us so often, and how almost every gay man has some level of internalized heterosexism. This helped to normalize his experience, prevent more shame (for allowing the internalization to happen), and create some self-compassion. Fred was now realizing that he was not a bad person for being gay, that there was nothing actually wrong with being gay, and that if society were not so fearful and narrow-minded, he could have been that singing kid without being punished for it. Eventually, as Fred continued to see that he was not the problem and felt less shame, he could see no longer feeling shame about sex with a man. However, he was still worried about not getting an erection and this concern was keeping him from engaging in the sex he deserved.

To deal with the erection issues, I explained to Fred that the more he thought about getting an erection during sex, the less likely it was going to happen. I showed him in session that if I told him to not think of a zebra, he was going to think of a zebra – that is just the way our brains work. And I explained that our bodies sometimes decide on their own how they are going to behave and just because parts of us behave differently than we would like, that does not mean they are dysfunctional or broken. They are just behaving differently than we would like. Fred having a better understanding of what was actually going on with his head and body, allowed further relief from shame. We then worked on ways to get him to be more present during sex, so he was not thinking of that "zebra". We explored Fred using his fingertips to touch a partner's body and really pay attention to how his fingertips were registering the other person's skin. This would help him to be more focused on his body than his brain and its anxious thinking. To help figure out other ways for Fred to be more in his body, and therefore more present, I asked Fred what especially aroused him when having sex. He mentioned being rimmed (having oral sex performed on the anus). I asked that when he realized he was caught up in thinking during sex that he ask his partner(s) to rim him and during it to truly pay attention to how all the nerve endings at his anus were responding to a wet tongue. We also discussed Fred having every right to communicate with his partner(s) and to take a break from sex for a few minutes, if he was too in his head about having to get an erection. These tools eventually allowed Fred to be less worried about an erection (which, of course, led to erections being easier and more frequent) and therefore more comfort in engaging in sex (even topping).

This comfort allowed Fred to be more realistic about his worth and to speak up with partners on how, in addition to anal sex and play, he received a lot of pleasure from frottage (sex that consists of rubbing the front of one's body against the front of another's body) and thought he would like to try receiving cock and ball torture (CBT). This led to him being able to experience these activities. With frottage, Fred would sometimes get erect during it and sometimes he would not, without feeling any major shame. He also realized that for him the fantasy of CBT was a lot hotter than actually experiencing it; however, he continues to experiment with different sexual activities that do not require an erect penis. And, more often than not, Fred feels whole and happy during and after sex with men.

Throughout the work with Fred, I made sure to, in my body, be aware of the sadness and anger I was feeling around what he had experienced as a child, being mindful of parsing out from our sessions what was my own trauma from childhood and when I could use those feelings to validate and connect with Fred. To process the anger around religion, I would remind myself that religion is not an all-or-nothing entity (it is not just good or bad) and that so many people do benefit from religion, while still holding space for how religion can be extremely damaging. I also discussed these feelings with my clinical supervisor.

Relational Therapy to Heal Attachment Issues

Because many gay men often experienced parents who did not know how to fully connect with a child who was not meeting their expectations, the parents' communication tended to be objective and have a "rational, from-the-outside-in, judgemental sense of things" (DeYoung, 2022, p. 60). This is a way of communicating that relies on the left brain, to the exclusion of the right brain (which is relational and emotional). This left-brain focus contributes to the insecure attachment that I mentioned tends to be common for gay men. My clients and I work to get them to be aware of their relational and emotional right brain. I encourage them to take tolerable risks toward trusting me to activate their right brain and connect with my right brain. In order to accomplish this with gay men, I have successfully used the guidance set out in DeYoung (2022):

• Healing happens when the client can experience a connection with their therapist where they see that a relationship with empathy and emotional joining is a real possibility for them.

- Because the parent was not able to reconnect soon enough (or at all) after telling the child they were bad, the therapist needs to be sure to look out for when the client is seeing themselves as either good or bad and make sure to stay connected with the client throughout those times.
- The therapist's curiosity of what is going on for the client must be partnered with empathy because we do not want to further objectify these clients and just come across as another voyeur judging them with our left brain.
- Since parents were not able to be "emotionally close to them and attuned to their needs" (p. 151), the therapist now provides this through the right-brain work of mirroring (reflecting back that the client is seen and worthy of love, regardless of the scale of their achievements), idealizing (having the therapist be a beacon of strength, opening a path for the client to have confidence in their own power), and twinning (the client having a sense that they are like and share similarities with someone else).
- Because the right brain is not fully developed, the more dominant left brain will verbally interpret what it understands the client to be experiencing. However, to get an actual read of what the client is experiencing, we will need to use our body language and pay attention to theirs.

Case Study

Juan is a 57-year-old, Latin, abled-bodied, gay, cisgender male, who uses he/him pronouns. He came to see me because he wanted to see why he had never been in a long-term romantic relationship and if he could learn how to be "better" at sex. As a Latin male, he felt pressure to be very sexual and dominant when it came to sex. He could not recall a time when he truly got pleasure out of sex and figured pleasure was not what he was supposed to experience since his "job" was to focus on being sexual and dominant. When we explored past attempts at establishing long-term relationships, I learned that Juan experienced a lot of anxiety once he started dating someone. If the guy did not reply within an hour of Juan's texts, then Juan would ruminate on whether or not the guy was actually interested in him, on a date with someone else, or was ghosting him. If the guy turned down an offer from Juan to go out, Juan would try to convince the guy to change his mine and spend time with him. If the guy still said no, Juan would spend that time he wanted to be with the guy alone in his apartment, anxious about what the guy was doing, and texting him to find out. Juan saw some of these behaviors as obsessive, but said he could not control himself.

When we explored his experiences around sex and I asked what he got out of sex, he had trouble answering. When I asked what he enjoyed during sex, he had trouble answering. And then he explained to me how sex for him is about making sure he is doing what he is supposed to in order to make sure that he is fulfilling his partner's expectations. Juan had decided that any man he had sex with picked him as a partner because they were expecting a "Latin lover", so in his mind, to keep the partner happy and still interested in Juan, he had to live up to their expectations. And Juan explained that often he did not want to have sex because he was worried he would "mess it up" and the guy would leave him.

Because of the intense fear he was experiencing around the potential for a partner to not stick around, we explored his childhood. Juan shared that his mother was around the home a lot and he would go to her when in distress. Sometimes she was able to help him feel safe and secure and sometimes she could not, leaving him to go to his room and try to ignore the situation he was in and the feelings he was experiencing. When Juan was an adult, he learned that his mother had a lot of anxiety and felt that there were a lot of times that Juan's needs as a child overwhelmed her and she had to take care of regulating herself, instead of attending to him. Juan's father was often working away from home; however, when he was at home, he did not interact with Juan, choosing instead to watch TV on his own or work out in the basement. Also, as an adult, Juan learned from his mother that she always thought his father was "bad at relationships".

Clinical Impressions

Since during childhood Juan's mother was sometimes available and sometimes not, it seemed that an insecure attachment was created for him and that this continued to be his characteristic style of attachment. As a child, his mother not being consistently there for him when he needed her likely seemed dire to him because he literally needed to rely on her for safety, security, and to survive. When he needed empathy, joining, mirroring, idealizing, and twinning from a parent, there were plenty of times that he did not get this from either parent and he must have felt extremely scared for his survival. Juan continues to see relationships through that childhood lens (of needing to rely on certain relationships in order to survive) and, as an adult, if someone does not make it obvious that they are there for him, he feels like his world is collapsing around him. Juan's brain and body did not realize that as an adult he no longer needed others as consistently as he had needed his parents as a child to survive. Not realizing this, he would go into survival mode in order to make sure a partner stayed around. And this included seeing sex as a device to keep a partner, something which filled him with performance anxiety, instead of being a way to receive pleasure.

I felt sadness for childhood Juan not getting his needs consistently met and for his parents not being able to fully connect with their child. I also felt sadness for Juan not yet realizing the joy that a fulfilling long-term relationship and sex that focused on his pleasure had the potential to bring. I was also fearful that Juan might become defensive of either parent or both parents if I started to shift responsibility for where he was today from himself onto them.

Treatment

I wanted Juan to ultimately take a risk and see what a secure attachment felt like. My guess was that his relational (right) side of the brain needed some attention in order to be more prominent for Juan. This meant me trying to ensure that my right brain was dominant and connecting with his right brain during our work together. Which, in turn, meant me especially looking for non-verbal clues about what Juan was experiencing because his right brain was likely going to be in survival mode when I tried to engage it, so what I would hear verbally from Juan would be his left-brain interpretations and I would be missing what was actually going on in his right brain. I worked to let my tone, facial features, eye contact, body language, and warmth do most of my communicating with Juan. Eventually, his right brain started to pick up on my desire to connect and see that I was able to do so consistently; in turn, his left brain was able to make sense of what his right brain was feeling, allowing him to continue to take risks in trusting and connecting with me. What I was doing consistently was mirroring, idealizing, and twinning. If his face showed fear of losing a partner because more than a few hours had gone by without hearing from the guy, I would reflect back his fear with my facial expression, and then change my facial expression to show a sense of determination and calm that he could trust my abilities to work through this with him, and I would support the message of being able to work through this by letting Juan know that for years I also dealt with overwhelming anxiety when I experienced guys I was dating not getting back to me when I would have liked, and how I survived these situations and he would too.

We also needed to work on distress tolerance during the times he did not hear back from guys when he wanted. What we discovered worked for Juan was texting a friend instead of texting the guy, seeing friends in person, dancing around his apartment, self-talk, and self-compassion. The self-talk and self-compassion consisted of Juan being aware of any grief around how as a child his needs were not consistently met, validating that his childhood brain was correct that he did need more from his parents as a child, and how he was struggling now because his current thoughts and feelings were based off a childhood way of thinking. Juan would remind himself that now, being an adult with his own resources and capabilities, he could handle some space from a partner or losing a partner and he would be just fine.

With a more secure attachment style, we began work on allowing him to take pleasure in sex. Juan was now open to the idea of enjoying sex for himself, since he was not as worried about pleasing a partner sexually in order to keep him around. We worked to debunk the myth that Latin men were all supposed to act in a certain way around sex and looked at sexual menus to have him decide on sexual activities he could see enjoying, trying, or staying away from. I also tasked him to determine which parts of his body were erogenous zones for him and how he liked to be touched – figuring a lot of this out during masturbation. He then took risks when having sex with partners by sharing with partners what he wanted out of sex, and found more of his sense of self and what was pleasurable for him. This was a crucial piece of his personality, further completing what it meant to be Juan.

In regards to my initial feelings, I used my sadness to connect with Juan, but worked to not let the sadness overwhelm me, and therefore Juan, by processing my sadness between sessions. I also used my fear of Juan becoming defensive of his parents to remind me to make sure I addressed how his parents were trying their best and were just human beings with their own coping and survival skills, even if, sadly, situationally he did not receive what he needed from his parents when it came to consistent and reliable feelings of safety and connection.

How We Can Help on a Broader Scale

We often feel as if as individual clinicians there is little impact we are able to have on a systems level. Some projects that I have taken on with success as a clinician to change the systems within the mental health space are: 1) providing a pro-bono consultation group for those therapists working with LGBTQ+ clients, 2) setting up a service to provide pro-bono therapy for LGBTQ+ clients by LGBTQ+ affirming and knowledgeable clinicians, 3) offering a lower fee in my private practice for those who are LGBTQ+ and BIPOC, disabled, or chronically ill, 4) providing training on LGBTQ+ related topics to local clinical agencies, including on sex and relationships, and 5) presenting informative lectures for school staff (including guidance counselors and nurses) on LGBTQ+ student and family issues.

We can also join or support existing movements. Here are some organizations that are helping gay men.

Aging

HelpAge USA – advances the wellbeing and inclusion of older people throughout the world's poorest communities
helpageusa.org
National Coalition on Aging – works to improve the lives of aging people by providing dignity, purpose, and health and economic security
ncoa.org

National Asian Pacific Center on Aging – preserves and promotes the quality of life of all diverse communities as they age, especially Asian Americans and Pacific Islanders
napca.org
Sage – provides advocacy and services for LGBTQ+ elders
sageusa.org

Disability Rights and Services Organizations

American Disabled for Attendant Programs Today – works toward gaining civil rights for persons with disabilities
adapt.org
Fireweed Collective – provides mental health education and mutual aid through a healing justice and disability justice lens for all people and centers queer, transgender, non-binary, and BIPOC folks in their internal leadership, programs, and resources
fireweedcollective.org
Sins Invalid – a disability justice-based performance project, centralizing LGBTQ/gender variant artists and artists of color
sinsinvalid.org

LGBTQ+ Mental Health

The Association of LGBTQ+ Psychiatrists
aglp.org
Gaylesta – The Psychotherapist Association for Gender & Sexual Diversity
gaylesta.org
Health Professionals Advancing LGBTQ+ Equality
glma.org
National Queer and Trans Therapists of Color Network
nqttcn.com/en
PFLAG – supports, educates, and advocates for LGBTQ+ people and their families
pflag.org
World Professional Association for Transgender Health
wpath.org

LGBTQ+ Rights and Services Organizations

The Ali Forney Center – in New York City, provides homeless LGBTQ+ youth multiple services to help them thrive and remain housed
aliforneycenter.org
The Asexual Visibility & Education Network

Asexuality.org

GLAAD – works toward fair, accurate, and inclusive representation in media of LGBTQ+ people

glaad.org

Hetrick-Martin Institute – provides direct services to LGBTQ+ youth and their families

hmi.org

Human Rights Campaign – fights to ensure that all LGBTQ+ people, especially those who are transgender, people of color, and have HIV, are treated as full and equal citizens

hrc.org

Southerners on New Ground – supports liberation of LGBTQ+ people of all races, classes, abilities, ages, cultures, genders, and sexualities in the southern United States

southernersonnewground.org

Trans Lifeline – a hotline run by the transgender community for the transgender community that offers emotional and financial support

translifeline.org

Transgender Law Center – a transgender-led organization advocating to change laws so that all people are able to live safely, authentically, and free from discrimination regardless of their gender identity or expression

transgenderlawcenter.org

The Trevor Project – provides a call, text, and chat option to assist LGBTQ+ youth with issues of mental health

thetrevorproject.org

Race-Related Rights and Services Organizations

Black Youth Project 100 – Black youth activists who work toward justice and freedom for all Black people

byp100.org

The Movement for Black Lives – creates a space for Black organizations in the United States to come together to determine the best way to make gains in policy and culture

m4bl.org

Race Forward – teams up with communities, organizations, and sectors in order to strategize on how to advance racial justice

raceforward.org

Showing Up for Racial Justice – brings together white people to join the fight for racial and economic justice

surj.org

United We Dream – those most directly impacted by the immigration experience are on the front lines contributing to strategies for change
unitedwedream.org

Sex Therapy Clinical Organizations

American Association of Sexuality Educators, Counselors, and Therapists (AASECT)
aasect.org
National Coalition for Sexual Freedom
ncsfreedom.org

Weight-Related Rights and Services Organizations

Association for Size Diversity and Health – focuses on weight-centered bias through education, advocacy, and community
asdah.org/what-we-do
Nalgona Positivity Pride – a disordered eating and body-positive organization dedicated to creating visibility for Black, Indigenous, and communities of color
nalgonapositivitypride.com
National Association to Advance Fat Acceptance – offers education, advocacy, and support to help make the world a better place for fat people
naafa.org
Nolose – is responsible for national and regional conferences and provides support and financing to help diverse fat LGBT, queer, same-gender-loving, trans, and sex-positive communities
nolose.org

Reference

DeYoung, P.A. (2022). *Understanding and treating chronic shame: Healing right brain relational trauma*. New York, NY: Routledge.

Chapter 13

Clearing Up Body Misconceptions and Enhancing Pleasure

Greater Internal Validation and Healthier External Validation

When dealing with gay men and body issues that get in the way of them engaging in or fully enjoying sex, I like to make sure they have a grounded understanding about how systems work to make sure we all have unrealistic and unhealthy ideas of how our bodies should look. These ideas often being led by companies wanting us to feel we desperately need their products to look "normal" and to be accepted. I then ensure my clients understand that they may be more susceptible to internalizing the toxic messaging around body image (as compared to their heterosexual counterparts) because as gay boys they likely struggled to learn how to internally validate themselves, because the world was telling them that they were inherently bad, and so they had to rely on external messaging in order to feel validation (Downs, 2012). We discuss how this can lead them to desperately want to present an extremely specific body type to the world to feel accepted, worth, and any form of validation. This helps them understand why they put such a heavy, unnecessary, and unhealthy emphasis on what others think of their body. These realizations help to normalize their experience (reducing shame) and understand that relief needs to come from internal validation and healthier external validation.

To begin increasing internal validation, we start with work on them seeing themselves more realistically, using self-compassion. I want them to truly understand that they have been unjustly treated by external forces and that they need to stop internalizing that treatment as a sign that they are a bad person and instead be compassionate toward themselves for the way they have been (and continue to be) treated by the outside world. To accomplish this, we explore and experiment putting into practice the concept of "discriminating wisdom" instead of judgment. According to Neff (2011, p. 74) the former "recognizes when things are harmful or unjust, but also recognizes the causes and conditions that lead to situations of harm or

DOI: 10.4324/9781003386322-14

injustice in the first place" and the latter "defines people as bad versus good and tries to capture their essential nature with simplistic labels." I then connect this to how we need to work on their self-appreciation, which is relating to what is good in them, instead of focusing on self-esteem, which is a judgment of worthiness and pushes us toward seeing ourselves as either good or bad, instead of just who we are (Neff, 2011).

To support a client in understanding how others seeing them as bad does not mean that they are actually bad, we work on helping them understand why others are likely to see them in this way. I explain that as human beings we have evolved to see difference as danger; it is this irrational thinking that leads so many to be afraid of what is different from them (Taylor, 2021). I teach how when we began as a species, those who were easily suspicious of new things would have an increased chance of survival because they would err on the side of avoiding wild animals, poisonous plants, and dangerous individuals. We live in a different world today, in terms of immediate threats to our survival, yet the part of our brain that sees difference as dangerous is still active and is telling some of us that if someone loves, has sex, or looks differently than you, then they are dangerous and therefore bad.

When my clients have some practice with self-compassion, we continue developing internal validation by challenging them to radically love themselves, using Taylor's (2021) Four Pillars of Practice: 1) Taking Out the Toxic, 2) Mind Matters, 3) Unapologetic Action, and 4) Collective Compassion. I will show you how I used these with a client in the below case study.

For healthy external validation I have them contact their friends and biological or chosen family to ask what it is about them that they like. I have them put all the attributes in a list that they can easily access. This helps them be able to see the list when they are not being kind to themselves; repeated exposure will help create and strengthen new neural pathways around the reality that they are not broken. I also acknowledge that they will likely have a difficult time believing the good things people say about them because it goes against the hard-wiring of "knowing" that something is fundamentally wrong with them, so their brain will likely want to filter out concepts that go against that with which they are already familiar. This awareness helps them to be careful of allowing filtering to automatically happen.

If I find that they are not ready to love their body, then I am open to focusing on body neutrality. Thus, instead of looking to have them radically self-love all of themselves, we focus on the parts of their body and aspects of themselves outside of their body that they do appreciate and discuss how they are all housed in a vessel, known as their body. They are then able to see how their body, by making possible a place for parts of them to reside, is taking care of them.

If my clients tell me that they only want to change their body because they are unhealthy, I make sure they understand the misinformation out there around health and body size, and I speak to them about what specific medical issues they know to be related to weight. After exploring this, we discuss how "weight is not what matters, healthy behaviors are what matter" (Nagoski, 2015, p. 165). We then check in on their relationship to food and I make sure they are aware of living a lifestyle in line with the Healthy at Every Size® (HAES) Principles: Weight Inclusivity, Health Enhancement, Eating for Well-Being, Respectful Care, and Life-Enhancing Movement (Association for Size Diversity and Health, n.d.).

Case Study

Jay is a 39-year-old able-bodied, white, gay, cisgender male, who uses he/him pronouns. He came to therapy looking to get himself "over the hump" of not having had sex in years. He was fat, and he knew fat people had sex, but he just could not believe that anyone would want to have sex with him because he was fat. He often stated that he would not want to have sex with himself, so why would anyone else. Jay would go on the hookup apps, chat with people who knew what he looked like and wanted to meet up for sex, and then Jay would not follow through – feeling too much shame around his body. He was fearful of being rejected once he actually met up with someone and they were able to see his actual body, not just pictures of his body.

He grew up as a child who weighed more than most other children his age and his family let him know that they thought this was a very bad thing because he should be like other kids. Inherent in that messaging was that he should also be straight – compounding his shame. According to Jay, he was "a fat gay kid", "a pariah". At first his parents told him that they were still going to buy the "bad" snacks he craved, and that he would just have to be "good" and have "self-control". When Jay would sneak snacks at night, he would be punished. Eventually, his parents decided to lock up the food, telling Jay that he could not be trusted.

As Jay grew up, he tried strict diets that would decrease his weight, but these also made him miserable. And, eventually, he would get back to a certain weight. He also tried overusing laxatives to reduce his weight and, in addition to this method being unhealthy, the weight loss from it was even more short-lived than occurred when dieting.

Clinical Impressions

Jay's thinking was irrational, as he knew fat people had sex and he had met guys on the hookup apps who wanted to have sex with him. This irrational thinking likely came from how much shame he felt about himself, which came from how he was treated as a child around his weight. I could see Jay as an adult thinking, "Who would want to have sex with a pariah?" I also figured that he was internalizing the bombardment of messaging telling society, especially gay men, that there are a limited number of body types that are actually desirable, and that anything different is wrong and bad. Knowing that sex offers a unique opportunity to explore and understand our bodies, I thought that Jay was missing a vital piece of the puzzle that could help create and increase the love he had for his body and himself.

I felt anger at Jay's parents for how they had handled his weight issues and his relationship to food. I felt sadness for Jay not realizing his full self because he felt he needed to stay away from sex for the sake of others. I also felt sadness over my own journey through being a single gay man and not having the "right" body type.

Treatment

We began work on having Jay be aware of the concept of self-compassion and then begin to experience self-compassion. I asked that he purchase the book *Self-Compassion* by Dr. Kristin Neff. In session, we would review the chapters he read at home, as well as going over those exercises from the book that were relevant to him. Jay was able to see how seeing himself as bad or good was way too simplistic to be a true way of seeing himself, or seeing anybody, and that he was easily seeing himself as bad because of the messaging around him (from family, peers, and media) that being fat meant being bad. Realizing that he was not just good or bad, led us to work on learning who Jay *was*.

I asked that he have his friends email him some aspects of him that they liked and contributed to them being friends with him. I wanted it to be via email so that he could easily copy and paste and have a master list of valuable aspects of himself that he could draw upon whenever he was feeling shame and having trouble validating himself for all that he did have to offer. We then moved on to have his body being one of those things he valued and could offer others.

I also asked that he read *The Body is Not an Apology* by Sonya Renee Taylor. We would discuss the book in session and we focused, in particular, on Taylor's (2021) Four Pillars of Practice. We started with "Pillar 1: Taking Out the Toxic" by working on realistic ways Jay could be intentional about his media intake, realizing how much shaming messaging he was surrounded by. This took the form of limiting his overall media intake and him being more consciously aware of the messaging from what he was choosing to watch. We also had him join certain groups on TikTok so that he could see more realistic messaging around bodies. We then began work on "Pillar 2:

Mind Matters" by getting rid of his old tapes, the old narratives that were created by others that had Jay see his body as bad. Jay was going to be the author of his story and decide what kind of relationship he was going to have with his body. With less negative and more realistic messaging about bodies, Jay was able to begin to see how his body was not automatically something that he should be ashamed of and needed to spare others from. He was open to learning for himself what was good for him about his body. "Pillar 3: Unapologetic Action" led Jay to begin to explore his body through masturbation, doing so on his own terms, under no one else's eyes. This also meant risking looking in the mirror, with new eyes, at his body, first clothed, then, eventually, fully naked. He would journal about these mirror experiences and share them in session. We then moved on "Pillar 4: Collective Compassion" by working to trust that others could see him the way he now saw himself. This meant being open to guys on the hookup apps actually finding him sexy and attractive and wanting to have sex with him. While it took some time on the hookup apps (wading through the usual pitfalls of these apps), he was able to find regular hookup partners that he felt comfortable enough with to begin exploring himself when it came to sex with others. He said that over time he was less concerned about how other sex partners felt about his body because he could "love it enough for the both of them".

At Jay's request, we then moved onto his relationship with food. On his own, Jay was able to see how he was replicating in adulthood what he learned in childhood about food. Food was bad, something he should not enjoy, and control himself from indulging in. As an adult, Jay, would find ways to keep food away from himself in his own home. He would eventually get to the food and eat it in greater quantities than he truly wanted, feeling shame about this and then eating more to deal with that shame. We worked on Jay talking to that childhood self and letting him know that his parents' unfortunate way of handling his weight led to unrealistic ways of understanding what food meant. He shared with that child how food can be pleasurable and nourishing and not just bad and harmful to one's body. Jay then started telling his adult self this, in order to now begin to eat with less shame. Eating without being anxious of what he was doing to his body had an additional benefit of improving digestive issues that Jay had had for years. Having better predictability around his digestive issues led to him feeling more comfortable bottoming during sex, which allowed him to experience a part of himself that wound up being integral to his identity.

To deal with the anger that I felt toward Jay's parents, I reminded myself that they were probably doing the best they could. I also held onto some of the anger in order to join with Jay around the eventual anger he would feel toward his parents and I allowed myself to keep some of the sadness around my own body issues present in order to join with Jay. While during our work

Jay was struggling with following through on sex, I did honor and hold space for my own sadness around what he was denying himself.

Transgender and Non-Binary Interventions

A group that may not be well served by the interventions shared thus far in this chapter are those who are gay and transgender or gender non-conforming. I have found that often their body issues are related to an incongruence they feel between who they are and what their body looks like. This could mean having curves, genitalia, a chest area, a voice, and/or body and facial hair that do not fit with their identity. With these clients, we look at how these specific issues may be getting in the way of sex and work to introduce and have them feel comfortable playing and experimenting with sex that is not genitally focused or helping them and then their partners understand that "the presence of a part should not necessarily lead one to presume than an individual wishes that part interacted with in culturally prescribed ways" (Fielding, 2021, p. 93).

Case Study

Liam is a 25-year-old, able-bodied, gay, white, non-binary person, who uses they/them pronouns. They came to see me for therapy because they knew they had a desire to have sex with men, but past attempts had not gone well, and they were now losing that desire. Liam was worried that they were "psychologically losing libido". This was causing them sadness, a sense of hopelessness, and had them question their sexual orientation and their overall identity, especially since before their affirmation/transition they were attracted only to women.

Liam shared that there were parts of their body they had dysphoria around. These included their chest and hip areas. And there were some parts they were completely fine with. These included their vulva, height, and arms. Since they did not have dysphoria around their vulva, they could not understand why they were having trouble enjoying oral sex by others on their vulva. They began to wonder if they were actually comfortable with their vulva, or if this was just something they were telling themselves. They had trouble seeing how they could be comfortable with their vulva if having it stimulated orally was not pleasurable.

Liam grew up in a typical household when it came to sex. Sex was only referenced as something they should stay away from until they were married or, at least, found someone they truly loved. Outside of that, sex was a dirty indulgence that should be avoided. And Liam never heard anything from their parents around masturbation; however, they knew it was important not to reveal they were masturbating.

Clinical Impressions

Liam was having a lot of doubt that was causing distress because of their misunderstanding around what leads to pleasure in sex, how common it is for people to fully realize their sexual orientation once they are able to transition/affirm their gender, and whether or not they had the right to advocate for themselves around sex.

I was angry at how their parents communicated sex to them and the systems set up to shame sex, especially for female-presenting children. I was sad that Liam was questioning their own identity over some likely misunderstanding about what they were "supposed to" enjoy about the sex they were having.

Treatment

We worked on making Liam aware of the narrative they had in their head around what their role in sex should be. They realized that they learned to be passive around sex because they did not want to be the one to be active and making decisions around something as dirty and taboo as sex. They felt they could absolve themselves of guilt and shame from sex, if they let their partner make most of the decisions. We had Liam go back and speak with their childhood self, to help them see that sex outside of a serious relationship was not inherently bad and that, when consensual, could provide a lot of benefits that they were deserving of. With bringing thinking more into reality around sex, Liam felt comfortable enough to begin to explore what role they fantasized about when it came to sex. They were able to see that there was a more dominant side to them that they were not exploring. Liam stated how they wanted to tell guys to, "Stop focusing on my extra hole and give my clit dick some attention!" When masturbating, Liam spent most of their time on their clit dick and that was how they would orgasm. By giving Liam an affirming space to talk about and explore sex, they were able to realize what they truly wanted out of sex and began to feel empowered enough to ask for it. Liam's better understanding of what they wanted from sex also provided relief because it did involve an attraction to men, helping them feel less conflicted about their identity.

However, they still questioned how comfortable they could be with their extra hole if they did not enjoy oral sex involving their extra hole. To address this, we looked into where this idea came from for them. They shared that people who do not have dysphoria around their vulva are supposed to feel stimulated and pleasure from oral sex focused on the vulva. I made them aware that they were letting cultural norms dictate a binary for them around how someone should and should not experience pleasure from certain body parts and what that means about their relationships with their own body parts. After figuring out how they wanted their extra hole pleasured, we opened this up to help them further explore what other parts of their bodies they wanted to bring into and keep out of sex, getting rid of societal expectations of what sexual acts are supposed to get you aroused. After work on figuring this out, we worked on exploring more of their dominant side during sex and how they would use this before and during sex to let partners know how they were going to be pleased.

The anger I felt around what was communicated about sex to Liam was a familiar feeling that I was able to process, hold onto, and bring into the sessions to some degree to join with Liam, creating a space for them to feel their own anger. I also held onto some of the sadness to join with Liam around the questioning of their sexual orientation and identity, while holding space throughout our process for the possibility that they actually were not interested in sex with men and that they had dysphoria around their extra hole.

References

Association for Size Diversity and Health. (n.d.) Retrieved December 30, 2022 from https://asdah.org/health-at-every-size-haes-approach/

Downs, A. (2012). *The velvet rage: Overcoming the pain of growing up gay in a straight man's world*. Boston, MA: Da Capo Press.

Fielding, L. (2021). *Trans sex: Clinical approaches to trans sexualities and erotic embodiments*. New York, NY: Routledge.

Nagoski, E. (2015). *Come as you are: The surprising new science that will transform your sex life*. New York, NY: Simon & Schuster Paperbacks.

Neff, K. (2011). *Self-compassion: The proven power of being kind to yourself*. New York, NY: HarperCollins Publishers.

Taylor, S.R. (2021). *The body is not an apology: The power of radical self-love*. Oakland, CA: Berrett-Kohler Publishers, Inc.

Chapter 14

Managing Anxiety and Increasing Sexual Enjoyment

How Cognitive-Behavioral Therapy (CBT) Can Help Gay Men

When dealing with gay men who have anxiety and sexual issues I tend to lean on cognitive-behavioral methods. Empirical studies have shown how CBT may be helpful in treating sexual problems with gay male couples (Peixoto, 2022).

I begin by making sure that the client understands what stress is and how it can either help or hurt them. We identify what about the sexual situation(s) in general tend to cause stress for them. Then we look at what they believe are the benefits they are getting out of being worried and at what cost they are gaining these benefits. From this exploration, they are generally able to see that anxiety is needed in sex, but that too much will get in the way. So, we look to find the balance that works for them by assessing what current techniques they use to manage stress and what we could add to those. Then we work to bring thinking into reality around their specific stressors. We explore the source of the anxiety, the negative beliefs about themselves and/or the situation that are contributing to that source, and what they know about themselves and/or the situation that go against their negative thinking. From this exploration, we find more realistic beliefs with which to go into sexual situations. To assist in this process, I often will have the clients use an Evidence Record worksheet, where they write out a specific negative thought and then list the evidence for and against this belief. I ask that they revisit the sheet over a few days, to provide fresh thinking, and then we review it in session. From the sheet they are able to more clearly see their cognitive distortions contributing to unrealistic negative thinking. I also have them make sure the sheet is easily accessible so that they can be reminded of this more realistic thinking when they are caught in a negative cycle of thinking.

How the Dual Control Model Can Help Gay Men

I also find explaining and exploring their particular dual control model to be illuminating and that it alleviates a lot of stressors related to sex. I use Nagoski's (2015) way of laying out the model:

DOI: 10.4324/9781003386322-15

- The central nervous system being a pairing of accelerator and brakes
- The brain system that controls sex also having a pairing of accelerator and brakes
- A part of the brain is always scanning internally and externally for sex-related stimuli that will add up to being turned on, seeking sexual pleasure, and another part of the brain does this scanning for aspects that will be a turn off
- This scanning is happening on a subconscious level
- Which stimuli wind up turning us on or off is unique for each of us, being learned through culture
- The work is changing what the brain responds to when it comes to sex, not actually changing the nervous system pairing of accelerator and brakes

When my gay male clients understand that there is an innate system at work in their body that everyone has to deal with, there is a normalizing that tends to provide great anxiety relief. Helping them understand that they need to pay attention to their turn-offs, not just what turns them on, also lessens anxiety because it gives them hope around what the future of sex could be for them now that they are paying attention to the whole system responsible for arousal.

After explaining the dual control model, we work on exploring what unique stimuli activate their accelerator and brakes. In this chapter, Worksheet 2 (also available on this book's product page at www.routledge.com/9781032478715) can help with this. We take each of their turn-ons and look for ways to enhance these before, during, and after sex. When focusing on what typically contributes to turn-offs, I start with how their five senses might gather information that turns them off. I then move on to other aspects, such as body image, internalized homophobia, shame, performance anxiety, childhood development experiences, trauma, and current daily and life stressors. We then explore how we can change thinking, perceptions, or behaviors in order to allow some easing off of the brakes.

How Sexual Menus Can Help Gay Men

If one of my gay male clients is having issues with a particular body part during sex, we will set up a menu of ways that person can experience sensuality without using that body part and can include anything from intercourse, to feeling sand between their toes, to watching leaves blow in the wind. In this chapter, Worksheet 3 (also available on this book's product page at www.routledge.com/9781032478715) can help with this exploration. According to Iasenza (2020), this type of menu allows the client to start seeing themselves as a sexual being without having to include a certain body part. I have found creating this menu does take the pressure off sex being so narrowly defined and relying on just certain body parts. This lessening of pressure does tend to allow those body parts that were issues to become less of an issue or no longer an issue at all.

When creating these menus for my clients with erection issues I work to free them up to list items that authentically speak to where they are sexually by attempting to take the pressure of erection off the table. I explain that the penis is just another body part that will not always behave the way we would like and so we cannot be wedded to the idea that erection equals arousal or that we need an erection to have pleasurable sex. There are many times throughout the lives of people with penises that erection occurred spontaneously/without arousal, or, alternatively, when they were aroused but not erect. I hope the client is able to take this information and use it for self-talk when there is a discrepancy between how their penis behaved and how they wanted it to behave – being more realistic in their thinking and feelings. We discuss and validate how it is fine to be disappointed but unrealistic to see themselves as failing, because that is not what is occurring (Klein, 2012).

Another bit of information I want to make clients aware of in order to more easily prepare their menus is that most of us learned about sex, what we liked and didn't like sexually, and what our bodies were capable of sexually when we were teenagers and young adults; as we age, these preferences and abilities will change (Klein, 2012). I caution them against automatically filling up their menu with sensual turn-ons and desires that were only connected to a younger self and body.

Pain Management

After exploring physiological explanations for anodyspareunia (pain during receptive anal sex), we will often find that anxiety is leading to the experience of more pain than is actually occurring or causing them to tighten their sphincter, which leads to pain. We want our clients to be aware of any real pain that is occurring as tearing of tissue and bleeding are very real potential outcomes of anal sex. Also, it is very likely that they will feel some sort of initial pain or discomfort while their sphincter is adjusting to an object entering into it. I teach my clients to pay attention to the real pain that is happening in their body, instead of the thoughts that cause them anxiety, so cause them to tighten their sphincter, which in turn causes them unnecessary pain. These thoughts could be "This is going to be extremely painful the entire time" or "I am dirty for having sex with a fourth new guy this week" or "I am not going to be able to take his cock and he is going to think I am bad at sex" or "Oh. God. Please let me have douched enough". We work on them being aware if they are focused on thoughts of potential upcoming pain or that any pain they currently feel will continue or get worse. If this is the case, we shift thinking to prioritize the actual pain that is there and then paying attention to when there is no pain. This requires the client to be very in touch with their body, so that they are able to distinguish between actual physical pain and what the brain may be trying to convince them that they need to worry about. This connection to the body starts with daily activities (like walking barefoot around the house, putting on body lotion slowly, and paying attention to the water hitting their body in the shower) and then moves to daily mindfulness exercises of body scans.

A lot of gay men will use poppers to help them relax overall, making it easier to be penetrated. Poppers usually come in a small jar; they are alkyl nitrites that are inhaled one nostril at a time with the effect being a quick high during sex. This drug is not regulated by the FDA and is often marketed as a cleaning supply so that it can legally be sold in the United States. Actual consumption by a person of poppers is not legal in the United States. Mixing poppers with alcohol use or medication to help with erection can be very dangerous.

Case Study

Sam is a 31-year-old abled-bodied, Black, gay, cisgender male, who uses he/him pronouns. He came to see me because he was feeling insecure around establishing relationships. He thought guys were not interested in him because he was not "performing in the bedroom" so he wanted help being able to perform. He stated he was having trouble reliably getting and keeping an erection and also being able to receive guys anally. He was looking for tips on how to fix these two things right away. I let him know that typically they were no quick fixes, because the causes were likely varied and we would need to investigate, figure them out, and then look to work on them.

Sam grew up in a household with two brothers. During his childhood, he experienced his father favoring his two brothers and being quite verbally abusive to him. His brothers displayed typical male attributes of being into playing and watching sports and, in adolescence, constantly talking about and coming around with girlfriends. The two brothers also happened to be conservative-leaning in their political beliefs, as were both parents. Sam's father was known to have a temper and could be a bully, especially if he was drunk, which would occur at least once a week. Sam would often seek refuge in his room, alone, when his father was on a tear about something going on that the father did not like. When what he did not like involved Sam, Sam isolating in his own room was not an option. His father would come in and be blatant about how Sam was not doing well enough in school, needed to have more friends, needed to start dating (girls), and needed to join sports teams in order to be in better shape (as he was "skinny like a girl"). Sam had moved away from this abusive environment when he 18 years old; however, for financial reasons, he had to move back home with his parents and that was where he was living when we started working together. They lived in a conservative suburb.

Sam was relying solely on the hookup apps to find people to date. He stated on his profile that he was looking to date and would run into a lot of people asking him if had or "was" a BBC (big Black cock) and expecting that he would top. This was shame-inducing for Sam because he did not know whether or not he wanted to top and his penis size was average. When he did find people that might be a fit, he would chat with them for a few weeks before meeting up with them. He felt comfortable on the dates; however, when it came to sex, he was very anxious about this being where the person would come to see Sam as a failure (his penis too small and not good at topping) and no longer be interested in him. However, he attempt to top because that was expected of him by partners and he felt self-conscious about bottoming, even though he often fantasized about it. However, since he could not always count on an erection, that gave him enough of a push to try bottoming. Here he also had trouble as he was having difficulty being penetrated without severe pain.

Clinical Impressions

Sam had a lot of insecurity and false beliefs around what it meant to be masculine, and also his own masculinity. This thinking was keeping him from being open to receptive anal sex, as it is often seen as feminine. These same concerns around masculinity, in addition to not actually wanting to top, may have been leading to the erection issues. It also seemed that Sam was having difficulty enjoying his sexual experiences because of his negative filtering, personalizing, mind reading, and future telling.

I felt sadness because, like so many others, he had grown up in a household with parents who have their own unprocessed issues around masculinity and sexual orientation, and wind up taking out their own lack of knowledge and insecurities on their children who are not a prototype of what a man is supposed to be. And I was feeling some happiness because, while he was not focusing on them, there were times when Sam did enjoy sex.

Treatment

After discussing starting with his primary care physician to see if there were any medical explanation for the issues around erection and anal insertion, I validated the racism and stereotypes that he had to deal with and the systems that needed to be overcome in order to be his authentic self. We discussed average size being average for a reason and how that meant he was more likely to be that size than any other size, regardless of his race. I also normalized the toxic nature of the hookup apps, while working through the very real emotions of shame, sadness, and anger that treatment on the hookup apps was creating for him.

We continued to explore his childhood and I provided psycho-education on how in childhood there is hard-wiring created by a small, but rapidly growing brain that will allow us to have irrational ways of seeing things that get stuck in our heads for a lifetime, if we do not rewire. I also explained how we were going to use CBT to help him rewire his brain. We used an Evidence Record to have Sam target irrational and unrealistic thinking around what it meant to be a man (addressing his negative filtering) and what was more likely a reason for a guy deciding to no longer see or date Sam (to address his personalizing). I had him simply fold a piece of paper in half vertically, put his very specific negative thought at the top of the page, and write evidence for and evidence against that belief. To address the beliefs that the guys he was dating saw him as puny, feminine, and bad at sex we used a CBT sheet focused on mind reading which allowed Sam to write down what he was thinking others were thinking of him and discussed how what he wrote down might be him projecting his own thoughts about himself onto others. He was able to realize how the other person could be thinking so many other things, and how he might feel better about himself if he were more realistic about not putting his own insecurities in the thoughts of others. To deal with future telling that dates were not going want to see him again after the first date or after sex and that he would not be able to be erect or receive anal sex, we worked on a CBT sheet that let him see how he has been wrong in the past around what would happen around dates and sex, how he can remember this when next time he thinks he can predict the future, and how he can notice when he is engaging in future telling, in order to curb the behavior. For each of these sheets I asked that Sam fill them out over a few days, so that he was coming to them from different mind sets and that, once completed, he kept them in an easy to access place so that he could easily retrieve and read them when his hard-wiring was kicking in.

As CBT helped Sam re-evaluate how he saw masculinity and his own self-worth, he was able to feel more comfortable around the idea of bottoming, not seeing anything wrong with wanting to be penetrated. This eventually led, with some teaching around breathing, relaxing, and lube, to Sam being able to bottom and thoroughly enjoy bottoming. The more realistic thinking around masculinity also led him to realize that he was just looking to top in the past to prove that he was a man, and now was not concerned about needing to prove this with an erection and being able to top. We realized that he may have had trouble with erection because the idea of topping led to his brakes being put on. In addition to the bottoming, we created a menu for Sam that included other sexual activities that might bring him pleasure that did not involve his penis being erect. Eventually, Sam started to have a lot more erections during sex (likely due to new beliefs and less focus on performance), so we also came up with a menu of sexual activities that he wanted to try when he did have an erection.

I used my sadness around my thoughts about Sam's parents to help Sam also feel sad that his negative thinking and irrational thoughts were products of his parents' own insecurities and unfortunate misguided thinking that they were actually doing what was best for Sam. We used this sadness to gain self-compassion for Sam and compassion for his parents who did not grow up with enough confidence or realistic way of seeing things to allow them to embrace and celebrate, instead of shunning, a child that was different than what they expected.

Treating Sexual Compulsion

For those gay men suffering anxiety due to a belief that they have a sex addiction, we explore the myths and realities around the concept of sex addiction (as mentioned in Chapter 2), assess whether there is a sexual compulsion issue, and, if there is a sexual compulsion issue, we treat that compulsion. We would do harm to clients by using an addiction model of treatment related to issues around sex. An addiction treatment model would mean keeping them away from anything related to sex, dictating what is healthy and unhealthy sex, and/or advising that they join a 12-step program and this would not be effective or ethical treatment (Neves, 2021). Of the 12-step programs related to the idea of sex addiction, please be aware that Sexaholics Anonymous (SA) is extremely heteronormative in what it defines as healthy sex.

I have found that Neves' (2021) assessment for sexual compulsion is a helpful tool with my gay male clients. The elements of this assessment that have been especially relevant are exploring the intensity and frequency of the urge, what happens after the urge, the ability to control the urge or the sexual behavior it may lead to, if the urge gets in the way of any life functioning, and what has occurred in the past if they have tried to resist acting on the urge?

After some assessment, I also use Neves' (2021) suggestions for interventions and have found that exposure management and identifying and making up for life deficiencies tend to work especially well for treating gay men. Instead of working furiously to avoid thinking or acting on urges, I encourage my clients to welcome the urge, because it is already there. We find where it is in their body, have the client describe what it feels like, and ask that feeling what it needs for relief. Often the client will realize that what they need for relief or satisfaction is not sex-related. This leads us to work on identifying areas of their life that they wish they were more fulfilled in. I explain to them that the sexual compulsivity is trying to make up for other areas of their life where they feel deprived and then list the areas identified by Neves

(2021) that tend to make a fulfilling life: "health, work, family of origin or family of choice, friendship and meaningful connections, romantic love, fulfilling sex, passionate engagement, a sense of belonging, finances, a sense of awe" (p. 72). Once areas have been identified by the client, we work on ways to directly get more fulfilment in those areas.

If the client continues to have trouble with the urge or behavior, then I have found grounding exercises work well to get them to be mindful of where they are and all that is going on around them, so they do not stay stuck in their head believing that they need to pay attention to this urge and that there is only one way to satisfy it. This grounding may be asking them to look out of a window and notice what they see, or looking around the room they are in and identifying the color of objects, or sitting through a mindfulness exercise where they feel their feet fully planted on this earth. This tends to bring them back into reality and feeling a strong enough foundation to have better control over their urge.

Case Study

Gabe is a 54-year-old able-bodied, white, gay, cisgender male, who uses he/him pronouns. We were already working together in therapy when Gabe let me know that he had a "serious confession" to make – he was a "sex addict". He explained to me that most weekday nights and at least once a weekend, he was finding or reconnecting with someone on Grindr and having sex with them. He spent most of his time away from work on his own and he did not like how he felt when he was alone. Alone, Gabe would ruminate about how he continues to fail being in romantic relationships and, while he had a lot of friends, he felt they were just not enough to help him feel whole. So, instead of torturing himself with rumination, Gabe would get on Grindr. Looking for someone to hook up with in itself was a welcome distraction for him. Meeting up for the hookup and having sex was a pleasurable distraction for Gabe. He would get home exhausted and with a smile on his face, easily able to fall asleep. However, the next day he would have the same urges to distract to get out of his head and avoid his feelings and would get back on Grindr. Gabe shared great shame around having sex so often with different partners and then further shame because he felt he could not stop himself from doing it.

Like most of us, Gabe grew up in a family that encouraged boys to "toughen up" and get over their feelings, especially those of sadness. Crying was *verboten* and met with punishment (often by making Gabe be by himself to "have time on his own to pull himself together") and his parents getting dysregulated (usually yelling at him). It was very scary for little Gabe to see those he relied on to survive and wanted to connect to, be less stable, and distance themselves when he showed what he was experiencing internally.

Clinical Impressions

A childhood of learning that paying attention to feelings provided devastating results and when he did something "wrong" he should keep himself away from others stopped Gabe from being vulnerable enough with others to have fulfilling relationships, including with himself. He also seemed to be going to the hookup apps in order to avoid feelings that he actually needed to be paying attention to.

I felt sadness that he internalized messaging that having a certain amount of sex and partners meant that he was automatically doing something he should be ashamed of. I was also sad that we continue to live in a society where the idea of vulnerability being weaknesses is taught to children.

Treatment

We worked immediately to take the judgment out of sex (regardless of frequency and partners) through helping Gabe realize that he was taking societal cues to slut-shame himself and would not feel the same way about a friend if that friend was having sex the way Gabe was. We then dispelled the myths around sex addiction and assessed to see if Gabe may have a compulsion that he wanted to work on. He had already shared the frequency of the behavior and then explained that it could take him up to five hours sometimes to find someone on Grindr and have sex with them. I was already aware of the shame he felt after he followed through with the behavior (as he thought it was feeding into his "addiction") and that his past attempts at not going through with hooking up had not kept him from the behavior. In terms of life functioning, while it was helping him get to sleep, it was also taking away time that he could be spending experiencing and processing his feelings or with friends. The actual sex itself was completely consensual and he was not taking any risks with which he did not feel comfortable. It did not seem as if his job or other life areas were affected in any way.

We tried exposure management. During the evenings, when the ruminating was occurring, Gabe was to lie down and pay attention to what he was feeling in his body. He first described a small tornado feeling in his belly. We stayed with this and he was able to sit with the discomfort of the tornado and welcome it, since it was already there and ignoring it would not make it go away long-term. While still paying attention to his body, we explored what that tornado might need in order to slow down a bit and maybe just be some strong winds. He was able to ask the tornado what it would need and heard that it needed to be "smothered" to help it lose some of its power. The smothering wound up being Gabe rubbing his stomach and eventually hugging himself. He realized that he needed touch and compassion for the tumultuous feelings he was experiencing, instead of the distance from himself and shame that had historically allowed the tornado to pick up speed and have him feel as if he was a danger to himself and others. It took time and more exposure management for Gabe to actually be close and vulnerable enough with himself and his friends – taking small risks at first and seeing the rewards of those risks shaped his future behavior. For example, we started with his closest friend and had Gabe tell her that he was in therapy, what he had been working on, and ask if he could reach out to her when he was having an urge and, if she were around, go to her for some company and a hug. Gabe got to a point where he was still using Grindr to hook up, but not doing so in order to avoid the tornado when it would act up on occasion.

After processing on my own and with my supervisor, the sadness brought up by Gabe's case, I did share my sadness with him so that he could understand how much systems were to blame for what he was going through, and that he was not actually a bad person or doing something that was bad.

Working with Sexually Transmitted Infections (STIs)

Like other populations, for gay men the fear of getting a STI can contribute to anxiety around sex. I like to make sure my clients have the facts around STIs so that they can make informed and shame-free decisions around safer sex. I share how bacterial/parasitic infections are curable: chlamydia, gonorrhea, syphilis, crabs, scabies, and trichomoniasis. I let them know that if these STIs are treated early, curing them can be quite easy – typically a shot or round of shots or oral antibiotics. (An exception is that, as of the writing of this book, there is a strain of gonorrhea that is showing to be resistant to treatment.) We then talk about those STIs that are viral and not curable: HPV, herpes, HIV, and Hep C. The only exception to this is molluscum, which is viral but can be treated and does go away, even without treatment, in two to four months. I also make them aware that any bacterial STI will increase the risk of getting HIV due to the likelihood of broken skin, fluids, and a lot of white blood cells around the infected area allowing an easy entry for HIV.

Since STIs have the possibility of not showing any symptoms, I recommend my sexually active clients get a full STI screening every three to six months. For my gay male clients, I make sure that, in addition to the typical ways STIs are screened for, they consider testing for chlamydia and gonorrhea of the anus if they have recently bottomed or are bottoming and feel discomfort in that area and gonorrhea of the throat if they have given oral sex or rimmed and experience persistent throat discomfort.

I am also aware of how people with disabilities and chronic pain and illness are at a further disadvantage when it comes to awareness of STIs due to possibilities of not having sensation in certain body parts that would signal a possible STI or not having the privacy to check their body for STIs (Kaufman, Silverberg, & Odette, 2007). For these situations, regular testing and figuring out how much you can trust an attendant to help with checking has the ability to help (Kaufman et al., 2007). For more detail on safer sex practices for this population, I would recommend Kaufman, Silverberg, and Odette's *The Ultimate Guide to Sex and Disability* (2007).

When it comes to practicing safer sex, like most populations, gay men are not wild about wearing condoms. However, for a lot of gay men the idea of condoms can be wrought with shame and trauma. Starting with the AIDS epidemic, condom usage was strongly touted as what a "responsible" gay man should easily wear when having sex. However:

> Because [gay men] were human beings, the condom…was often forgotten or dismissed in the altered consciousness of sexual arousal. [Gay men] would feel deep shame about this behavior, and they would conceal it from others…Condoms were also a lurking reminder of the lethality of sex, and a significant physical and emotional barrier between two men who were trying to connect.
>
> (Odets, 2019, p. 89)

Because of this potential added layer of difficulty around using condoms for gay men, I do explore how my clients feel about wearing condoms and see if we can untangle any associations between condoms and shame and trauma. I also work to let them know that through this untangling I am not pushing them to use condoms, nor am I judging their decisions around condom usage. I also use Odets' (2019) suggestion of making Negotiated Safety an option, as it has shown to have efficacy in the long term as a risk-reduction method. This is when partners make an agreement that they will let the other(s) know if they did something to put them at risk of an STI. While not foolproof, it can offer some protection for those who choose not to use condoms.

For those who are open to using condoms, I share some tips they may not be aware of that can make wearing a condom more appealing and safe. These include:

- Origami and pleasure dome condoms allow more freedom of movement and a feeling more similar to not wearing a condom than your typical latex condom.
- Adding a few drops of lube on top of the penis before putting on the condom will help with sensation when the condom is on. This should be just a few drops because too much lube will increase the chances of the condom coming off.

- Rough Rider condoms have bumps in the condom that help with stimulation.
- Use lubricated condoms because non-lubricated condoms will likely absorb whatever lube was used on it and inside the receiving party.
- Any silicone-based lube will increase the likelihood of a condom breaking.
- Receptive condoms are also an option and can be used on the anus by removing the inner ring of the condom.

To further decrease anxiety around STIs I explore with my clients the usage of pre-exposure prophylaxis (PrEP), their right to have conversations with sexual partners about STIs and testing, and making decisions during sex that are in line with their safety goals by not allowing alcohol or drugs to negatively affect their decision making.

Treating Sexual Abuse Trauma

> Sexual violence often doesn't look like "violence" as we usually imagine it – only rarely is there a gun or knife involved; often there isn't even "aggression" as we typically think of it. There is coercion and the removal of the targeted person's choice about what will happen next.
>
> (Nagoski, 2015, p. 124)

For my gay male clients who have experienced sexual trauma, having sex can lead to re-traumatization, a lowered sense of self-worth, issues with erection, anodyspareunia, dissociation, and/or flashbacks during sex.

People with disabilities are at a higher risk for sexual assault because of exposure to unknown caretakers and disabled children being seen as victims that are less likely to tell about or be believed about the abuse (Kaufman et al., 2007). This, of course, does not mean that we assume that a person with a disability has been sexually abused. But I think it is important to be aware of this higher potential and the situations that tend to lead to it.

It is not uncommon for gay males under the age of 18 to have sexual encounters with males substantially over the age of 18. When initially exploring their sexuality, adolescents can find men older than them offer an opportunity to learn about sex from an experienced individual. Also, with the hookup apps, the majority of males under 18 (lying about their age in order to be on these apps) will, by far, have mostly men significantly over 18 as options. While this age difference does fall under the category of statutory rape, a lot of gay adolescents are not traumatized by these interactions because they were able to go into these situations with enough autonomy to consent and be grateful for the experience. So, if a client shares experiences like these, I do not automatically try to force them to believe that they have been raped. Instead, I inform them of where one tends to be typically in adolescence in their ability to make decisions and consent and explore with them their actual experience of sex with older men.

When I have been told or suspect that trauma has been experienced, I have found that an updated version of the PLISSIT Model (Permission, Limited Information, Specific Suggestions, Intensive Therapy), which emphasizes permission and the therapist having a sense of self-awareness throughout the therapeutic process, does work well with my gay male clients. Following the guidance of limited information, during my assessment I do not ask about details. Details could serve to retraumatize the client and for some could come across as if you are trying to determine how severe the abuse "actually" was – which could be extremely invalidating and potentially trigger them by reminding them of others who did not believe them. However, if they want to tell their story, then that is extremely important and I do make space for them to do so. Also, during my assessment I make sure they are aware that sexual abuse does not need to involve violence, and is about coercion and lack of consent. After getting my usual background on their family of origin, childhood development/current hard-wiring, and attachment style, I will have a conversation with them and look to get a general understanding of the nature of the trauma(s), how it has impacted their functioning, if they know if it has impacted how they are able to experience sensuality, previous therapy focused on the trauma, and current coping skills.

We need to work to ensure that the client is able to cope with whatever may be triggered during our work. So, soon after learning about current coping skills and ensuring they are being practiced, we strengthen those existing skills and look to see if we need to build new skills. If we need to develop new coping skills, then we will look to build from the client's existing strengths and habits. One skill I tend to explore with clients is slowly getting them to be in touch with their body. We slowly work our way up to an in-session body scan, starting with the options of, at home, bare feet, lotion on the skin, and showering mindfully. If during the body scan, they get triggered, we go back to the previous body part they were experiencing in order to go back to a safe place and ground them. Then I check in to see if they would like to revisit the part that triggered them or end the exercise for that session. If they do want to revisit, we go back to it more slowly than we were going previously. And to help avoid shame or the need to perform, I let them know that if they do not feel anything in their body, that is common and a show of how much the brain is trying to protect them, and we will just need to give the brain some more time to realize that they are safe now. When considering use of the body scan, I am aware that "many members of marginalized groups, including trans and non-binary folx, don't often experience many feelings of safety in their bodies" (Fielding, 2021, p. 114). So I may not use it at all or be extremely slow when using it, depending on the client's particular situation.

If the client is not currently in an abusive situation, I do a lot of work with these clients to separate the past from present. While validating their current and past feelings and experiences, I try to make it clear that the trauma they are experiencing now is based on memories and what the body is holding onto. We work on mindfulness to get them to have body and mind more situated in what is actually happening for them in the present.

Most survivors had control taken away from them during the assault(s), so having a sense of control is crucial to their recovery. I always want to do my best to help them feel a sense of control – from the pacing of sessions, to how physically close I get them, to all decisions being theirs. However, this need for control can get in the way of experiencing sexual please because one has to give over some control (be vulnerable) in order to turn themselves over to pleasure. So, when the client feels ready, I work with them on still feeling ultimately safe, while relinquishing small incremental bits of control over time during sex.

Also, most survivors (especially of childhood sex abuse) will likely initially blame themselves for the abuse. As long as they hold onto the false belief that they were responsible for what happened to them, the work to heal themselves will be difficult to impossible. Why would they truly want to work toward helping the one they feel caused their trauma? So, we work to help bring thinking into reality around who is to blame. One way we work toward this is making them aware of the, often not mentioned, fawn response. Like any other response to being in survival mode, fawning can automatically kick in when in danger. Fawning will have them do what they are able to appease their abuser in order to try to escape less harmed. Understanding fawning as instinctual tends to help them be more realistic about what actually happened during the abuse. I also find the "friend technique" effective here. I ask them to think of a friend and then if they would blame their friend for the abuse the way they are blaming themselves. Very often they see that they would not and begin to understand why it does not make sense to take on the responsibility of being abused.

After the initial assessment, working on coping skills, separating past from present, and paying attention to control and blame, I then work with these clients to get a better understanding of how they see sex. "Survivors need to develop new attitudes about sex in the early stages of sexual recovery work so they can see it as being something positive and worth pursuing" (Maltz, 2012, p. 272). I assess whether the client is comfortable using the idea of consensual and pleasurable sex as a measure of good sex, and, ultimately, a goal for us to work toward. If they are, then we do work on finding out where they are comfortable being touched (for help with this, please visit this book's product page at www.routledge.com/9781032478715 and view Worksheet 4) and what they find pleasurable, arousing, and sensual. I will explore these areas by helping them determine how their five senses respond to sensuality and being creative when creating sexual menus because I want them to open themselves to not just considering what they have been told or have learned sensuality needs to be or involve. Because of the greater need to provide a space where these clients can have control, when working on a menu to list what they find arousing, we move very slowly when adding items and if I make suggestions of possible additions (in order to give them options they may have not considered), they are those that I feel are safe based on what I know about the trauma.

I also am very aware of the client having control when it comes to using sensate focus with my gay male survivors: "Sensate Focus is a set of touching suggestions that serves as a powerful therapeutic approach for helping people experiencing sexual concerns" (Weiner & Avery-Clark, 2017, p. 3). Sensate focus sessions tend to be singular events that are timed and then journaled about. This allows the pace to be intentionally slow and the client to be able to reflect on their experience, detailing what worked for them and did not, and us to discuss this work in their therapy sessions. The touching suggestions per event are very specific and typically start fully clothed and do not include touching of the genital areas. At the client's pace, future events could include less clothes worn and touching of the genital area. The idea is to build up to what is tolerable and pleasurable for the client. Sensate focus was introduced by Masters and Johnson (1970) and continues to be an effective tool in general for sex therapy. If you are not already familiar with sensate focus, I recommend that you at least read Weiner and Avery-Clark's *Sensate Focus in Sex Therapy: The Illustrated Manual* (2017) or take a class on its application. Examples of ways to adapt sensate focus that I have seen work for gay male survivors is for them to decide on the pace, length, and hierarchy of touch, pick the location in the home and what degree of clothing they have on during the exercise, include breathing exercises and self-talk if they choose, and decide who will have their eyes opened or closed (Weiner & Avery-Clark, 2017).

If the client shares or shows that the sensate focus protocol is not where they are, I will explore some touch exercises that may feel even safer. I typically will use these Maltz (2012) exercises, in this order:

1 "Sensory basket: The survivor interacts with a basket of sensual objects – such as an orange, spices, velvet cloth, a feather, silk fabric – one at a time while paying attention to smells, textures, colors, tastes, sensual feels, and so on" (p. 277).
2 "Drawing on the body: The survivor writes a message, letter by letter, on the partner's back, making a sweeping gentle hand stroke across the back between each word" (p. 277).

3 "Red light–green light: The survivor looks at and then touches specific places on the partner's body, for limited periods of time, using a start-stop protocol for controlling touch" (p. 277).

Another great option for trauma survivors, and anyone dealing with great anxiety around sex, is the use of a surrogate sex partner. The surrogate partner, the client, and the clinician work together to devise a plan that includes the surrogate being active with the client to better understand what is occurring for them physically and emotionally around sex and then work toward creating and enhancing skills that will resolve these issues. Please be aware that the legal status of surrogate partners is not clearly defined in the United States (and most other countries); however, the American Association of Sexuality Educators, Counselors, and Therapists (AASECT) has recognized surrogate partners as an effective and ethical part of the therapeutic team since 1978. If your client feels that this is an option they would like to explore, I would suggest you start with surrogatetherapy.org.

Case Study

Noah is a 39-year-old abled-bodied, white, gay, cisgender male, who uses he/him pronouns. He came to see me because he had a history of sexual abuse and was sure that it was somehow getting in the way of him being able to fully enjoy his life, including his sex life. After the first incident of abuse by a friend male, in early adulthood, Noah became very isolated, distancing himself from other gay male friends and only speaking with family and a few male friend. He felt a sense of loss from giving up his community of gay men, but felt he needed to experience this loss in order to feel safer. Noah was still engaging in sex with men that he would meet through the hookup apps and was very excited to be exploring some kinks that he had fantasized about. These kink spaces became the only places where Noah could feel safe with gay men. He enjoyed being submissive and felt safe because of all of the consent, communication, and checking in involved with kink. He began to believe he might be able to transfer some of these behaviors to his life outside of sex in order to create agreements with gay male friends that would allow him to feel safe. But before he could put this into practice, he experienced another incident of sexual abuse, this one very loosely associated with kink play. After that experience, he resolved himself to just have female friends and his family (having moved back in with them after the second attack). Noah felt as if he was losing parts of himself by not being around other gay men and, even more so, by not being part of the kink space, and wanted to see if therapy could facilitate his feeling safe enough to re-engage with each.

Clinical Impressions

Since kink was a space where Noah could engage with gay men and have that lead to considering engaging with gay men outside of sex, it seemed possible that kink may be his way back on the path of trusting again. We would obviously have to take things slow, be very careful not to re-traumatize Noah, help him feel a sense of control throughout the therapeutic process, and see if he would be comfortable with sex as a tool to heal.

I felt happiness that there was something that had worked for him (kink) that we could attempt to go back to as a way forward and a sense of hopelessness when I heard that kink became an unsafe space for him. And I felt anger at and sadness for the people who abused Noah – knowing they likely had their own troubling pasts that would lead them to such behaviors.

Treatment

Throughout our session I wanted Noah to feel a true sense of control. I looked to accomplish this by letting him know verbally (stating to him that we will be going at his pace), my actions (actually taking his lead for pacing, so continuing to check in with myself to make sure I was allowing this to occur), and my body language (reading his body language and asking permission in terms of my distance from him before, during, and after the sessions).

First, I learned about previous coping skills. Noah shared that after the first sexual abuse incident he sought out therapy and learned box breathing to help him regulate himself. Box breathing starts with breathing out slowly, getting all of the air out of your lungs, then breathing in through your nose slowly for a count of four, holding your breath then for a count of four, exhaling for a count of four, holding your breath again for a count of four, and repeating all of that for a few more rounds. We relied on this to get him through any times of being dysregulated. We also added a safe space exercise for when we would attempt body scans. Noah liked to imagine being at the beach. I would encourage him to take in the smells, sounds, sights, and feelings he was imagining around him.

After having coping skills in place, I asked Noah to share what he was comfortable sharing, and that the actual details were not important and how telling them could be re-traumatizing. He shared that the first assault happened in his early 20s when he was sleeping on a friend's couch and woke up to find the friend giving him oral sex. This led Noah to universally see gay men as people he could not trust in relationships, since a gay male friend (someone he had a close relationship with) could harm him. This led him to get rid of current gay male friends and not look to make others. The second assault took place when he agreed to kink play with two men. He met up with these two new guys for sex who said they liked some of the same kinks that Noah was into. When he got to their place and began negotiating what the scene would be, he was able to get a sense that they were new at this. As previously mentioned, Noah got to a point where he was considering transferring his comfort in the kink space with gay men to spaces outside of the kink space. So, he decided to have sex with the guys, but told them that there would be no kink scene during their play. The two guys agreed; however, they did not honor that agreement and after this violation of Noah, he no longer felt safe enough in the kink space to re-enter that world. Throughout the telling, I made sure my face and body language were letting him know that I felt his pain and horror and then that there was hope to continue to survive and thrive.

I wanted to get a sense if he blamed himself for these incidents, because that would likely lead to shame, and that shame would likely lead to obstacles in him feeling deserving of thriving, or even surviving. He shared not blaming himself for the first incident, as he had no reason not to trust sleeping around his friend. He did, however, blame himself for the second incident. He felt that he should have left when he got the sense that the guys misled him about their experience with kink. He believed he was just being "slutty" by having sex with them as an alternative to kink play, and that maybe he deserved what happened because "kink was risky business."

We worked on bringing his thinking about who was to blame and the safety of kink into reality. We explored if he would blame a friend of his who went into the same situation he did with the two guys and this allowed Noah to begin to see that he did not do anything wrong by engaging with these two men and his consent was violated. This reinforcement in his mind that his consent was violated also allowed us a window into Noah recalling that for those who are truly kinky, consent is vital and valued as a priority. These two men were not truly part of the kink community.

We next worked on how Noah could be more aware of how this past trauma was still living in his body. He was already somewhat in touch with his body, so body scans early on were useful. I first led him in basic mindfulness of sitting with his feet on the floor, palms up on thighs, eyes open, and slightly looking down and about six feet in front of him, an upright back posture (as if an invisible string was pulling him up), and paying attention to his regular breathing. Then I asked that he start with his toes and make his way, slowly, up to his head, scanning for any sensations in the bodies. If he got to a place that caused discomfort, he was to try the safe space exercise – escaping to his calm place and trying to see, hear, smell, and feel what was around him. Two areas that Noah identified were his chest (over his heart) and his shoulders. He felt emptiness in his chest and a heaviness in his shoulders. We worked to ask these areas what they might need for relief and his chest let him know that he needed to reach back out to friends that he had disconnected with and his shoulders let him know that he needed to stop working so hard to keep himself away from aspects of the world that were actually good for him. After a few sessions digesting this information and making sure Noah was feeling safe, we began talking about reaching out to the gay male friends he had let go of. He was open to the likelihood that at least some would be happy to hear from him, and could understand, have compassion for, and forgive his dropping out of their lives.

We also began talking about re-engaging in sex, particularly kink, as this was so fulfilling for him. While rationally he knew that the two guys did not represent the true kink community, his body was not allowing him to experience the type of play with which he had previously connected. I asked and he said he was open to lighter and slower versions of his typical play. He asked one of his past regular play partners if they would be willing to go on this journey with him and they consented to it. They worked on this play with Noah fully clothed and discussed the very specific areas that were to be touched and not to be touched. Noah also decided how long the sessions would be, and would journal after each session – sharing and processing his entries in his therapy sessions. Before any of this play started, we also rethought his aftercare plan, to see if he might need it to be different in any way because of this way of re-engaging in play. An aftercare plan is part of kink negotiations and speaks to how each scene partner will want to be cared for after the scene. Noah did not wind up needing to change his. Over time, Noah slowly let his partner know when touch could be increased and when other areas of his body could now be lightly touched. He also decided the pacing of how much he would be dressed and was able to get to a place of wearing only what he was wearing when he played before the second assault. Eventually, Noah got back to the level of intensity in his play that he was at previously. At this point, Noah appeared before me as a person I had never met. His posture, face, and body language conveyed confidence. He realized that while the trauma may not fully leave his body, he did not need to let it take over and he could know it was an impression from the past that was part of his story, but not a defining aspect.

I made sure to explore my hopelessness and, when I did, realized that it did not have a place in the sessions, and would not serve Noah. I was able to have hope, and bring that into the room, when I made myself clearly aware of how many resources Noah had at his disposal to deal with these traumatic events. I used my anger and fear toward the abusers to help Noah see that it was appropriate to be angry at these men, while understanding that they too likely have been hurt in order to behave in such a way toward others – holding space for anger and compassion.

References

Fielding, L. (2021). *Trans sex: Clinical approaches to trans sexualities and erotic embodiments*. New York, NY: Routledge.

Iasenza, S. (2020). *Transforming sexual narratives: A relational approach to sex therapy*. New York, NY: Routledge.

Kaufman, M., Silverberg, C., & Odette, F. (2007). *The ultimate guide to sex and disability*. San Francisco, CA: Cleis Press, Inc.

Klein, M. (2012). *Sexual intelligence: What we really want from sex and how to get it*. New York, NY: HarperCollins.

Maltz, W. (2012). Healing the sexual repercussions of sexual abuse. In Kleinplatz, P.J. (Ed.), *New directions in sex therapy*. New York, NY: Routledge.

Masters, W., & Johnson, V.E. (1970). *Human sexual inadequacy*. New York, NY: Little, Brown and Company.

Nagoski, E. (2015). *Come as you are: The surprising new science that will transform your sex life*. New York: Simon & Schuster Paperbacks.

Neves, S. (2021). *Compulsive sexual behaviors: A psycho-sexual treatment guide for clinicians*. Abingdon, Oxon: Routledge.

Odets, W. (2019). *Out of the shadows: Reimagining gay men's lives*. New York, NY: Picador.

Peixoto, M.M. (2022). Affirming diversity and targeting pleasure: Sex therapy for gay male couples. In R. Harvey, M.J. Murphy, J.J. Bigner, & J.L. Wetchler (Eds.), *Handbook of LGBTQ-Affirmative couple and family therapy*. New York, NY: Routledge.

Weiner, L., & Avery-Clark, C. (2017). *Sensate focus in sex therapy: The illustrated manual*. New York, NY: Routledge.

Worksheet 2: "No, Thank You" and "Yes, Please"

There are many factors that could keep us from wanting to engage in sex and also a ton that could arouse us. If you are looking to increase your frequency and/or quality of sex, it is important to be aware of as many items as possible that may lead to turning you off or on.

Give some thought to what gets you out of and into the mood for sex, and make a list below.

Environmental factors (examples: smells, noises, lighting, people around you)

No, Thank You   *Yes, Please*

_____   _____
_____   _____
_____   _____
_____   _____

Stressors (examples: work, children, parents, politics, safety)

No, Thank You   *Yes, Please*

_____   _____
_____   _____
_____   _____
_____   _____
_____   _____

Thoughts (examples: false beliefs about our bodies, how deserving we are of intimacy, or how well we need to "perform")

No, Thank You   *Yes, Please*

_____   _____
_____   _____
_____   _____
_____   _____

"No, Thank You" and "Yes, Please" (Continued)

Emotions (examples: sadness, happiness, anger, fear, love, guilt)

No, Thank You   *Yes, Please*

_____   _____
_____   _____
_____   _____
_____   _____

Other factors

No, Thank You   *Yes, Please*

_____   _____
_____   _____
_____   _____
_____   _____

Worksheet 3: Sex Menu (Blasting Off to Another Dimension)

There is various messaging we have received on what sex is supposed to look like, how long it is supposed to last, what body parts we are supposed to focus on, and that we need to end sex with an orgasm. I am letting you know that you can free yourself from the sex you are "supposed" to have and have the sex that actually stimulates you and provides you with pleasure.

Imagine that you are in another dimension where no one tells you what your sex life is supposed to look like, but, instead, each being is allowed to decide for themselves what they would like to happen during sex. As one of these beings, write, draw, say out loud, tell yourself, or in some other way they communicate in this dimension, share what you want your sex to look like.

Chapter 15

Decreasing Depression and Substance Reliance and Increasing Pleasure

Dialectical Behavior Therapy (DBT) to Treat Gay Men

Linehan (1993) created the only therapeutic methodology to date proven to work with people living with Borderline Personality Disorder, DBT. Early in my career I worked at a mental health clinic that was part of a foster care agency. At this clinic, we were trained in DBT because a lot of the clients, both children and adults, were diagnosed with Borden Personality Disorder. Later in my career, when I started my own practice, focusing on the LGBTQ+ community, I realized that a lot of gay men could benefit from DBT. I wondered if this meant that a lot of gay men were living with Borden Personality Disorder? Over time, I was able to realize that since those diagnosed with Borden Personality Disorder typically were severely invalidated as children and this was a common occurrence for most gay men, skills that help someone better trust their internal self to regulate themselves and connect with others (like those taught through DBT) were going to help gay men.

While I make use of the four core skill areas (Mindfulness, Interpersonal Effectiveness, Emotional Regulation, and Distress Tolerance) explained in Linehan's *DBT Skills Training Handouts and Worksheets* (Second Edition) (2015), there are certain skills, and corresponding worksheets, that I find work especially well with gay men, who have been invalidated in childhood for not behaving the way a parent expected a boy to behave. These skills are:

- Wise Mind
- Nonjudgmentalness
- Recovering from Invalidation
- Practicing Self-Validation
- Identifying Values and Priorities
- Body Scan Meditation
- Practicing Mindfulness of Thoughts

DOI: 10.4324/9781003386322-16

Wise Mind

I have found that Wise Mind helps balance out brains that have become overly focused on being rational in order to avoid having to deal with the hurt and shame they experienced as children or overly focused on their emotions defining what is going on for them because as a child they spent so much time experiencing but never processing their hurt and shame. To help them get a more realistic sense of what their feelings and thoughts are trying to communicate to them, so that they are able to achieve Wise Mind, we work on being more mindful of their body and thoughts. I also present them with a worksheet from Linehan's *DBT Skills Training Handouts and Worksheets* (Second Edition) (2015) for practicing Wise Mind and have them pick two skills from it. Two popular choices being: 1) breathing in and completely focusing on the word "wise" and breathing out and completely focusing on the word "mind" and 2) breathing in and asking themselves if what they are currently thinking is making use of Wise Mind.

Nonjudgmentalness

With systems constantly and blatantly judging and criticizing gay men, it is no wonder that they easily will be judgmental and critical of themselves. Often times, my clients are not aware of how much they blame themselves for not completing a task perfectly or not meeting some impossible goal that they arbitrarily set themselves. I will use the "Would you judge a friend for that?" question to begin to get them to see how harsh and unrealistic they are being with themselves. Once they are aware of this, we begin to practice nonjudgmentalness from a worksheet of Linehan's *DBT Skills Training Handouts and Worksheets* (Second Edition) (2015) that provides a checklist of practice options, one example being "Write out a nonjudgmental blow-by-blow account of a particularly important episode in your day" (p. 89).

Recovering from Invalidation and Practicing Self-Validation

Gay men not being aware of how much they blame themselves allows a great toll to be taken on their bodies. Clients do not realize that with self-blame, often the body closes in on itself in order to make itself smaller, so the client can spare others of their "wrongdoing". I validate why they would feel that this is necessary and help them see that they are doing this with their body not because of something they did wrong, but because of them being invalidated by some societal dictate of how they are supposed to feel and behave. To recover from this, we have them make their bodies as big as possible. We pretend they are scaring off a bear. This opposite movement and posturing of the body does help them receive messaging counter to the idea that they are not valid and need to shrink. When they are aware of the invalidation occurring, we practice ways for them to validate themselves in situations, instead of assuming that the invalidation they are receiving must be deserved. To help with this, we complete a worksheet from Linehan's *DBT Skills Training Handouts and Worksheets* (Second Edition) (2015) which provides the client with a choice of alternate internal responses (to just blaming themselves) when being invalidated.

Identifying Values and Priorities

With so many outside voices telling gay men that they are leading immoral lives, it is no surprise that a lot of gay men would look to behave more in line with what society tells them is the moral way to be. I validate for these clients that changing their behavior to match the masses may seem like the best option, in order to avoid further shame, hate, and violence. Then we explore to see if their actual morals and values are amoral or hurting anyone else., Typically, the client has not allowed themselves the space to consider their own values and morals, due to fear of acknowledging something in them that is bad/goes against the larger society. Having them sit with how they actually feel about situations and want to behave and seeing it as "normal" provides a window for these men to not fear actualizing who they want to be and what they want to accomplish. With this new sense of being comfortable being who they are, we use a worksheet of Linehan's *DBT Skills Training Handouts and Worksheets* (Second Edition) (2015) that provides a checklist of values and priorities that are relevant to them that they may now feel freer to pursue.

Body Scan Meditation and Practicing Mindfulness of Thoughts

The overly focused emotional or rational thinking and taking in outside messaging that leads gay men to be hard on themselves and not be their true selves can all affect sex. This might play out with a person not being able to fully connect with someone during sex because they don't allow themselves to dive into their feelings to guide them around sex. Or it may look like someone letting their fear over not meeting some unrealistic expectation in the bedroom keep them from engaging in sex with others at all. To further help these clients pay attention to their bodies and what their actual thoughts are, I use one worksheet from Linehan's *DBT Skills Training Handouts and Worksheets* (Second Edition) (2015) which offers a step-by-step process for the body scan meditation (that I allow the client to record me reading while in session) and another worksheet that offers suggestions on how to observe, use words and voice tone, opposite action, and imagery to more easily be mindful of thoughts.

Removing Shame Through Self-Compassion

Having been constantly judged and ridiculed, gay men have internalized such negative messaging about themselves and experienced difficultly being able to have a healthy sense of self-worth. When one thinks they are not as good as others, their sex life is going to suffer, as they will likely be avoidant of sex either because they believe no one would want to have sex with them or because they worry that they will "fail" at sex. If they do engage in sex, they may not get pleasure out of it, feeling as if they are undeserving of any enjoyment. To work with this judgment, my gay male clients do well when they learn to distinguish between judgment and discriminating wisdom. We work to have them realize and understand that judgment is a too simple, unrealistic, way of labeling things as good or bad, while discriminating wisdom considers the reality of ambiguity, complexity, and how much situation plays a role in what happens in our life (Neff, 2011). To emphasize the reality of the complexity and uniqueness of individuals, we work to get them to accept that: "Being human is not about being one particular way; it is about being as life creates you – with your own particular strengths and weaknesses, gifts and challenges, quirks and oddities" (Neff, 2011, p. 79).

I also often make use of DeYoung's (2022) focus on restoring one's relationship with the self, which requires self-compassion and forming an inner self. "Shame begins as the feeling of self in broken relationship" (Deyoung, 2022, p. 36). A lot of gay men have been angry at themselves because they have not seen themselves as being good enough, or even good at all, so they have distanced themselves from themselves. To open a path to re-establishing a relationship with self, we need the client to stop being angry with the self and instead offer forgiveness and compassion. Deyoung (2022) points to the usefulness of Paul Gilbert's Compassion Focused Therapy's working to lessen a client's self-criticism so they can feel some warmth toward themselves:

> Negative emotions, internal conflict, and ambivalent feelings are normal, not shameful. Bad things that happen to us can leave us feeling undeservedly ashamed. Often we blame ourselves to keep ourselves safe in dangerous relationships. It's possible to make a bad mistake while being a good person. Instead of hating ourselves for mistakes, we can correct ourselves with compassion.

(p. 260)

Once the client's thinking is more realistic about being fine just the way they are, we work to specifically identify what systems have told them they are supposed to believe in, strive for, and behave like and determine how much of that is authentic to them. Once they see how much of who they are is based on what society dictated to them, we do grief work. We acknowledge the loss of not being their true selves for most of their lives thus far and process the pain of that loss. I share and we are guided by Nagoski's (2015) wisdom:

> The way to get through is to stay very still, to notice all the aspects of your identity that were tied to the lies you were told, to notice all the grief you feel in letting go of the self you spent your life trying to be. Notice, too, the anger you feel at having been lied to for so long. Notice all of these with nonjudgment. Allow them to be true.
>
> (p. 304)

Then we look to figure out who is their shame-free self. Once a gay man is able to free themselves from shame, then they are able to pursue contentment, which is made up of "passion, love, and integrity" (Downs, 2012, p. 155). Downs'(2012) explains that gay men can learn to feel passion by "creating and prolonging joy" (p. 160) and this is accomplished by making themselves vulnerable to joy, noticing when they feel joy, and repeating the behaviors that bring joy. One way we figure this out is the client creating their own scripts around what they want out of sex and sexual partners – making use of sexual menus and exploration of fantasies (as described in Chapter 10).

Reducing the Harming Effects of Religion

While there are many gifts that come out of religion, when it comes to gay men, there are often many hardships that it causes. The messaging of most religious institutions is that sex with other men is dirty and sinful. When I work with gay men who grew up in religious households, and for whom this messaging has brought great shame, our work begins with assessment and history taking around religion and spirituality. I have found some of Johnson, Rostosky, and Riggle's (2022) questions especially helpful in being better able to understand how my client was specifically affected by religion: what role it has in their lives, how intersectionality influences their experiences of and belief in it, how it helps and challenges them, what are their practices, what role did it have for them and their parents growing up, and were there any significant experiences related to it growing up.

After the initial assessment, I make use of Wolkomir's (2001) work with gay Christian men as my guide in successfully structuring treatment around the shame stemming from religion. Wolkomir (2001) has found that gay men need a safe space to share their dissenting views when it comes to how the majority see religion. They will often not reject outright all of what they have learned about religion, as it is often too tied to aspects of their identity.

While I try to ensure that my office is a safe place for dealing with issues around religion, clients tend to need more than just their therapist's office to get a true sense of validation. Sometimes clients can get more through joining an affirming religion and church. "Metropolitan Community Church, the Unitarian Universalist Church...and other affirmative faith-based groups support and validate LGB couples by recognizing couples and families and fully including them in spiritual life and leadership" (Johnson, Rostosky, & Riggle, 2022, p. 352). If they are not looking to be involved in religion or spirituality, then we look for local groups that provide a space for discussing religion and the LGBTQ+ community.

If a client is open to alternative ways to view religion, I try to shift the experience of religion from being about rules that need to be followed to more about what faith means for them in their hearts, reminding them of the love that can be present in religion and spirituality. I also see if they are able to view religion's purpose as finding their unique way, not just listening to a dominant authority's interpretation of "the" way.

When it comes to what religion has to say specifically about being gay, I share that there is a lot of misinterpretation of teachings of Christianity, Islam, and Judaism. For example, the story of Sodom and Gomorrah was more about rape, not being gracious and hospitable, and indiscriminate sex than it was anything related to sex between men.

Case Study

Jerry is a 67-year-old white, gay, cisgender male, with a chronic illness who uses he/him pronouns. He came to therapy because he was starving for human touch and wanted to "fix" himself so that he could go out and meet with others. Jerry is chronically ill and immunocompromised. He came to see me in 2021. Before the COVID pandemic, he saw the few friends he had on a semi-regular basis and enjoyed sex when he found partners that were a fit. Being considered an "old man" in the gay community had contributed to him being isolated – as he was having trouble finding gay groups that were welcoming and potential sexual partners that did not immediately ignore him because of his age. Since the pandemic, Jerry was now only seeing his mother in person and was feeling incredibly lonely and depressed. He felt so certain that he was not doing enough to force himself to be around other people and "failing at life". Jerry shared that his mother kept pushing him to do more outside the home, stating that he was just being "a scared little boy" and she wanted the best for him, so he should just go out and do things with others. He explained to her that he had already looked into local activities of interest to him, but there was no requirement for people to wear masks. She then informed him that "COVID is over". He thought he might be playing it too safe because he was too scared to meet and re-engage with others after being alone for so long.

Clinical Impressions

His mother had likely been this critical to Jerry his entire life. This would mean he would be hard-wired from childhood to see himself in a negative way. As a child, seeing himself this way would contribute to Jerry feeling that he had to "be better" in order to avoid behaviors that would create distance between he and his mother (whom he was relying on for connection, safety, and survival). That thinking was now causing him shame because he felt he was not doing enough to improve his situation in life.

I felt sadness for how COVID has affected us all and for how much more difficult it has been on those who are immunocompromised. Then anger set in at the politics around COVID and mask wearing, the idea that it is "over", and Jerry's mother being so critical and careless with him.

Treatment

I learned that, from an early age, Jerry started showing signs of experiencing great pain, lack of mobility, sensitivity to stimulation, and exhaustion. Doctors had difficulty finding a physical or biological cause, so they would say that it was likely something psychological that he was dealing with, not true physical issues. Jerry's mother fed into this belief and would tell him to calm down and say "it is all in your head" when he was experiencing an uncomfortable or painful episode.

Jerry was able to realize through sharing in session his childhood experiences of his mother that she took up a lot of space when he was a kid. She was very focused on her appearance and the décor of her home. A lot of the family finances went toward those two things. When Jerry heard about medical tests he could take to see what was going on for him, his mother would say they were not going to waste their money on that, since he just needed to toughen up and not be so "crazy".

We realized that Jerry had only a few friends because he did not feel deserving of their attention and that they would want to do things for and with him. He easily felt like a burden to them. So he would rarely initiate time together and would sometimes turn down invitations because he felt they were made out of pity for him. He felt the same about sexual partners and would only venture to "impose" on others for sex because he really needed some "release" and body contact.

We began by making Jerry aware that in order for one to see themselves and situations clearly and realistically they had to use both their emotions and rational thoughts in a balanced way, honoring each. He realized that his emotional mind was very strong and tended to dictate his perceptions. We worked on him, through self-talk, being able to give his, already existent, rational voice a bit more volume. We used breathing exercises to help remind Jerry to use his Wise Mind. With this new skill, we were able to attempt Jerry seeing that he had been doubted throughout his life by his mother and other authority figures, who were actually wrong, because Jerry did have physical issues, which were eventually diagnosed. He had such intense sadness around being doubted and invalidated, that his brain did not allow much space for him having been right about what was going on for him. We worked to have him realize and hold space for this. Within that space, we worked toward him having compassion for little Jerry, who was continually invalidated and criticized, and then to transfer that compassion to adult Jerry.

With the practice of self-compassion in place, we began to use DBT sheets that allowed him to identify new ways to react when others invalidate him (including feeling the pain, checking the facts, and not using self-talk that is judgmental), instead of him taking it in as evidence that he has failed (Linehan, 2015). We applied this directly to the thought that he had failed at having a social circle with which to connect. Through reality testing, Jerry was able to acknowledge that his thinking that the gay male community can be rejecting of those over a certain age and the risk he would be putting himself in if he went to certain events (due to COVID) was true. He was able to see how existing friends would not be incredibly put out by him asking them to test before seeing him and wearing a mask when with him – as they were likely taking tests often now anyway. Taking a risk and asking his friends to abide by these behaviors allowed Jerry to see his friends. This brought him much joy; however, Jerry shared that there was joy he was still missing out on – sex. He could get to a place of asking his friends to test but could not believe that a stranger who he meets on a hookup app would find him worth testing for. He applied his new skills, took a risk, and was able to find guys who were fine wearing a mask when Jerry came over and taking a test then, waiting for the results, and then having sex if they each tested negative. The sex he was able to have with his new sense of self-worth allowed him to explore new positions and activities that made sex more fulfilling and joyful. Experiencing this joy reinforced the belief for Jerry that he was deserving and a good person.

I used my sadness around COVID to join with Jerry, while validating that he was especially limited by the pandemic. And I used my anger to help him understand that he had every right to be angry with systems that were not caring about his survival and led to his mother being so worried about how others saw her that she was unable to see him.

Treating Substance Issues

When gay male clients are dealing with substance issues in addition to sexual issues, I want to first make sure that they know how certain substances affect sex. Most people are aware that alcohol can cause difficulty with erection. What they may not be aware of is that extended use of too much alcohol can cause nerve damage and alter hormones enough to disrupt communication between the pituitary gland and the penis, leading to permanent lack of erection. Some gay men will use the drug ecstasy in sex situations; however, this drug can actually cause difficulty with erection or get in the way of orgasm. Some gay men will use crystal meth to lower inhibitions and get more out of their sexual experiences. While this may be the case for some initially, continued use will have the opposite effect. It will eventually cause problems with erection, arousal, libido, orgasm, and getting overall pleasure from sex. Also, with crystal meth's initial ability to heighten comes an intense sex drive that could easily lead to high-risk sexual behavior.

If a gay male client wants to enter a 12-step program to deal with their substance issues, we do tend to look for LGBTQ+-specific programs, either in-person or online. General 12-step programs often center themselves around a spiritual or religious practice, which can be difficult for gay men, and can easily have in attendance people who are homophobic (Shelton, 2022).

Shelton (2022) puts forth two general frameworks for treating LGBT individuals experiencing substance use disorders: Trauma-Informed Treatment and Affirmative Therapy. I have shared in this chapter the tenants of trauma work that I find most effective with gay men. When practicing Affirmative Therapy, the basics are to not pathologize a client for being LGBTQ+, be careful of heteronormative bias, and have some knowledge of the LGBTQ+ experience.

To this I would like to add that the therapist not have an 'all-or-nothing' stance against drugs, projecting to the client that they only see the drugs as bad. For a lot of gay men the drugs help them lose their inhibitions, allowing them to push against societal boundaries, and this can be freeing for them to further express their gay identity and explore their erotic pleasures (Neves, 2021). I believe understanding a drug's positive aspects for this population is important in order for the client to feel validated and further trust their therapists.

Case Study

Cam is a 47-year-old able-bodied, white, gay, cisgender male, who uses he/him pronouns. Cam came to see me because he was often having trouble getting and keeping an erection with partnered sex and masturbation. From late adolescence until just a few years ago, sex was a great source of pleasure for Cam. He knew the kind of sex he liked and sex helped him to be in an internal space that he could not achieve outside of sex. However, for the past few years, he has had trouble being present and getting what he used to from sex. Part of this was due to trouble with erection. Cam explained that his head would be taken out of the game if he could not get an erection. Not being present for sex left him feeling some shame, sadness, and anger because he missed the vulnerability he was able to achieve with sexual partners. When we explored what may have occurred in his life that caused such a shift, what seemed the most significant was that his father died around the time this started happening. However, Cam did not see how the two events could be connected because he had a negative relationship with his father, so actually experienced relief when his father died.

Cam grew up in a household with two younger siblings, an alcoholic father who was verbally and physically abusive, and a mother who was likely co-dependent. Cam would "run interference" for his two siblings, and some-times his mother, when it came to the father's rampages – trying to get his father to calm down and take the brunt of his father's abuse. In addition to the many nights of physical violence and broken furniture, his father would shame Cam whenever Cam acted "girly". This treatment from the father only ended when the kids became adults and moved out of the home. As adults, family visits would consist of Cam being hypervigilant around how much the father was drinking (so he would know when it was time to leave) and masking (speaking with a deeper voice, making sure how he walked and sat followed societal masculine norms). Cam had decided he was never going to come out to his father. He did not want to give his father the "satisfac-tion" of confirmation that Cam was gay and therefore "less than". The father was drinking less during these times, likely because he was having related health issues and was not supposed to drink at all. Eventually, those health issues led to his death. Cam recalls feeling sad around the death, how-ever, this was more so because of the memories related to his father that were brought up for him rather than actually missing his father.

Clinical Impressions

His father's death triggered not only the past trauma of abuse, but also vari-ous elements of grief that had yet to be processed, including not being allowed to have a childhood (being parentified) and no longer being able to resolve his feelings about his father with his father.

I felt sadness for what Cam had to endure for his entire life and the child-hood he was robbed of. I was also experiencing anger toward, and sadness for, his parents, as they did not take care of Cam the way he needed and this was likely due to their own sad stories of childhood. I was also happy to know that up until the death of his father, Cam was able to get joy and realize part of his identity through sex.

Treatment

After having Cam see his primary care physician about his erection issues, I followed my typical model of trauma work. We made sure Cam felt in control of the sessions, letting him know verbally and through body language that I was taking his lead and continuing to ask for permission as we moved along in our sessions. We worked on existing coping skills and then developed and practiced new ones. While speaking to coping skills, Cam shared that he did start to drink a bit more once his father died. He thought this was a result of him feeling more relief and a sense of freedom, allowing him to enjoy more alcohol. He insisted it was not "a lot". Since "a lot" is relative, I asked for actual amounts, and it did not seem an excess of alcohol. Over time in our sessions, Cam shared that he had actually been drinking more than he originally disclosed, hiding the amount because he had shame around anyone knowing how much he was drinking. So much so, he would get up early on the days that the truck came to collect recycling so that he could bring out his recycling right when they showed up. He did not want the neighbors seeing how many empty alcohol and wine bottles he was getting rid of. I did not further shame him for his drinking levels; however, I did let him know that it was an unhealthy amount to be putting in his body, that it was likely causing some of his erection issues (even if he was not drinking right before sex because of the long-term effects of alcohol on organs), and that his increased drinking after his father died may have been an unconscious effort to avoid feelings, instead of anything celebratory. He was open to all of this.

We explored where Cam was placing the blame of what happened in his childhood. He shared that in childhood he blamed himself for not keeping his family safe; as an adult, however, he realized that he was just a child then and his parents were responsible for doing more to take care of the family. As an adult, he also realized that they likely suffered their own traumas which led to their behavior and choices.

Taking work at Cam's pace and with his coping mechanisms at hand, we used a picture of 6-year-old Cam to help him grieve the childhood that he deserved but did not get. This process allowed him to realize what that kid, like every other kid, needed to experience in childhood and how that did not happen for him. Realizing this allowed him to be able to have further compassion for his childhood self and what he had lost. To begin to process grief around his father's death, we went back to how he felt in his body when he received the news, and when he went through the ceremonies and rituals related to mourning. He had trouble recalling any feelings in his body, which

I normalized. However, he was cognitively able to understand that his father's death could trigger him around his trauma, as the father was the source of the trauma, and how he could grieve no longer having his father around to be able to process that trauma with and show his pride of being gay. This allowed Cam to work toward being more in touch with his body and eventually in session he was able to pay attention to how his body currently felt about his father. To get relief from what he was feeling in his body, Cam felt a deep need to know why his father treated the family the way he did (was he also hurt as a child) and if the father had any remorse. Cam then was able to feel and process the grief he felt in his body for never being able to get these answers.

Through therapy, Cam was learning more about how his father's death actually affected him and was even more open to the idea that drinking was a way to escape, not celebrate. However, he had become reliant on it to cope. We explored harm reduction and abstinence and Cam decided that he wanted to be sober because he felt alcohol was too easily addictive, considering his current habits and possibly inheriting alcoholism genetically from his father. We explored what he was getting from the drinking and Cam was able to realize it was a way to turn his mind off and relax his body. I validated the need for this and we talked about him working with a psychiatrist to see if medication might help provide this in a more consistent and healthier way. He wound up first trying Wellbutrin because the psychiatrist thought it could be effective and also because it was unlikely to have side effects that would get in the way of Cam figuring out how to once again enjoy all that sex provided him. We also worked on active mindfulness to help his thoughts not wander and relax his body – mindful walking, brushing of teeth, eating, and paying attention to what was in the room. He spent more time with friends, asking that the nights they spend with him were dry, which they easily complied with (many appreciating a dry night). He also found an LGBTQ+ AA meeting that he felt comfortable in. He thought his sponsor to be a great resource.

As he remained sober, we began to figure out what the obstacles to sex might be. He had started to get erections again when he was masturbating. However, he had high anxiety around these erections being able to transfer to a situation when he was having sex with others. I validated and normalized the concern. In addition to creating a menu of sexual activities that did not involve an erect penis, we explored the reality that our bodies may not behave the way we would like them to, pointing out that this does not mean something is broken; it is just how our bodies work. Not seeing himself as inadequate helped provide some relief. Cam also realized how much, since his death, his father had been (figuratively) in the room when he was having sex. This meant that perhaps Cam was having more trouble with enjoyment of sex because the increased presence of his father during sex led to more shame, sadness, and anxiety, especially around his sexual orientation. He was open to the grief work he already accomplished, leading to his father not being such a force in his mind when having sex. We also worked on him being more present during sex by paying attention to his senses during sex, especially how his palms and fingertips felt against a partner's skin. He took what we worked on and risked engaging in sex with others. After some trial and error with mindful focus during sex and bringing into reality some of the anxiety that was still present during the first few sexual experiences, Cam was able to accept the lack of reliance on an erect penis, be more present, and get back to enjoying a space that was unique in its ability to allow him to be him and get enjoyment that he deserved.

The sadness and anger I felt for Cam's childhood experience and related to his parents I processed on my own and decided to allow to be in the room at a low level to give him the option to also feel sadness and anger toward what he lost and he experienced with his parents. I used my happiness around his history with sex to allow hope to live in the room during our sessions.

References

DeYoung, P.A. (2022). *Understanding and treating chronic shame: Healing right brain relational trauma*. New York, NY: Routledge.

Downs, A. (2012). *The velvet rage: Overcoming the pain of growing up gay in a straight man's world*. Boston, MA: Da Capo Press.

Johnson, S.D., Rostosky, S.S., & Riggle, E.D. (2022). Where should we go to church? Or should we even bother: Spirituality and religion in LGB couples' therapy. In R.S. Harvey, M.J. Murphy, J.J. Bigner, & J.L. Wetchler (Eds.), *Handbook of LGBTQ-Affirmative couple and family therapy*. New York, NY: Routledge.

Linehan, M. (1993). *Cognitive-behavioral treatment of borderline personality disorder*. New York, NY: The Guilford Press.

Linehan, M. (2015). *DBT training handouts and worksheets*. New York, NY: The Guilford Press.

Nagoski, E. (2015). *Come as you are: The surprising new science that will transform your sex life*. New York, NY: Simon & Schuster Paperbacks.

Neff, K. (2011). *Self-compassion: The proven power of being kind to yourself*. New York, NY: HarperCollins Publishers.

Neves, S. (2021). *Compulsive sexual behaviors: A psycho-sexual treatment guide for clinicians*. Abingdon, Oxon: Routledge.

Shelton, M. (2022). Treating LGBT couples experiencing substance use disorders: Trauma-informed and affirmative therapy approaches. In R. Harvey, M.J. Murphy, J.J. Bigner, & J.L. Wetchler (Eds.), *Handbook of LGBTQ-affirmative couple and family therapy*. New York, NY: Routledge.

Wolkomir, M. (2001). Wrestling with the angels of meaning: The revisionist ideological work of gay and ex-gay Christian men. *Symbolic Interaction 24*(4), 407–424.

Chapter 16

Improving Intimacy

I like to start off my work with gay male relationships letting them know that they have some advantages over heterosexual mixed gender relationships. Being "less constrained by traditional and cultural scripts", they are more open around sexuality; and, perhaps because they typically know what it is like to have a penis, there tends to be greater empathy and less blaming when issues happen around erection (Peixoto, 2022, p. 122). If this is the case with the clients I am seeing, then we make sure to work from these strengths.

Treating Arousal Issues with Gay Men

Normalizing is extremely therapeutic and works wonders with sex because people often do not talk about the sex they are having, so there is nothing real with which to compare their sex lives. If relevant, I start by debunking the ideas they have around how the trajectory of sex and arousal are supposed to look. Most of my clients feel that sex is "supposed" to start with a spontaneous desire to jump on top of their partner and then end with orgasm. This is what they believe, and they have shame around doing anything that does not fit this model. I help them see that that is an outdated and unrealistic model of how sex works, especially with persons in long-term committed relationships. I like sharing the more realistic alternative of JoAnn Loulan's Sexual Model, which starts with willingness (not spontaneous arousal) and ends with pleasure or shutdown (not orgasm) (Iasenza, 2020).

I break down for them how arousal actually works. I explain that, contrary to popular belief, sex is not a drive, so sex does not need to rely on spontaneous arousal in order to happen. Without the presence of new relationship energy, when they are in the beginning of a new relationship and their brain is flooded with oxytocin and dopamine, there is less spontaneous arousal happening. When the new relationship energy chemicals wear off and they are living together, sharing in household duties, and learning more about the things that annoy them about their partner(s), they are less likely

DOI: 10.4324/9781003386322-17

to want and have the energy to just all of a sudden look at their partner(s) and want to have sex with them. Add on to this the unlikelihood that each of the partners would feel aroused and have the energy for sex at the same time. However, all is not lost. Quite to the contrary. There is a wonderful and often reliable alternative: responsive arousal. This involves being open to the possibility of sex when their partner or partners are aroused or when they have scheduled time to have sex. I advise they start the play and see if they wind up getting turned on. If they do, great, I suggest they keep on going. If not, then they stay where they are comfortable or stop altogether – always being aware of what they are comfortable with and want to consent to.

To help increase the opportunities for responsive arousal to occur, I typically recommend planning sex. While often not popular with clients, because sex is "supposed" to be spontaneous or else it is less special, they do wind up realizing that planning increases the chances of sex actually happening. When trying to figure out the times when sex is most likely to happen, we look to work within what time of day each partner tends to be most in the mood for or open to the idea of sex. Then we get very specific about how we are going to remove as many obstacles as possible from getting in the way of the sex date happening. This may be taking into consideration what is happening with children, pets, relatives living with them, time for douching (if anal sex will be involved), doing what tends to get them aroused and avoiding what tends to turn them off beforehand, and having zero expectations of what that time together needs to look like. For help with this planning, please visit this book's product page at www.routledge.com/9781032478715 and view Worksheet 5.

Also, when discussing arousal, I make sure they are aware that it is natural to go through periods where desire is dormant (Perel, 2007) and ask that they believe the partner's words when they tell them that they are turned on instead of relying on whether or not their penis is erect.

Increasing Vulnerability

Perel (2007) shares that the challenge of sexual intimacy is:

> …bringing home the erotic. It is the most fearsome of all intimacies because it is all-encompassing. It reaches the deepest places inside us, and involves disclosing aspects of ourselves that are invariably bound up in shame and guilt. It is scary, a whole new kind of nakedness, far more revealing than the sight of our nude bodies.
>
> (p. 104)

I have shared how this fear is intensified for gay men because of their childhood and adult histories of keeping distance from other men in order to remain safe and connected. So I always explore how vulnerable my clients are allowing themselves to be during sex and then work on building trust and vulnerability. The trust piece is often built up by paying attention to and reminding themselves of how their partner(s) have been there for them in the past. The vulnerability piece may happen through sensate focus (as discussed in Chapter 14) or a version of sensate focus suggested by Iasenza (2020), where touch happens between the partners with mindful, slow, and flat hand touches that are contained within a certain amount of time and then journaling to get at the thoughts, feelings, and bodily sensations that occurred. They then use this information to learn how they can slowly become more vulnerable and allow themselves to pleasurably receive the touch that they want.

What Makes Great Sex May Be Surprising

Kleinplatz et al. (2009) found that even across different sexual orientations, conceptualizations of what contributed to great sex in a relationship were very similar:

- Being present, focused and embodied
- Connection, alignment, merger, being in sync
- Deep sexual and erotic intimacy
- Extraordinary communication, heightened empathy
- Authenticity, being genuine, uninhibited, transparency
- Transcendence, bliss, peace, transformation, healing
- Exploration, interpersonal risk-taking, fun
- Vulnerability and surrender

(pp. 5–9)

I share this list with my clients and we discuss how different it is from what society and media tell us contributes to good sex. We then look at how many of these elements are already present for them and what they would like to work on.

Pearls of wisdom from Perel (2007):

- While equality of roles may prove healthy when it comes to other areas of the relationship, when it comes to sex, equality may not be necessary and could actually lead to boredom; try playing with power.
- When new relationship energy has run its course, create novelty by seeing your partner through different eyes and being open to not knowing them as well as you think you do.

- If you become fused with your partner, connection can no longer happen because there is no longer space to connect through, instead you are one person.
- You want to create some healthy distance, then bring that space to life – like a fire, desire also needs air.
- You must be comfortable asking for sex just because you want it; it is acceptable and important to be "selfish" in this way when it comes to sex.

I share this list with my clients and we review their thoughts and feelings about each of these points and explore whether they want any of these points as goals. If they do, then we create a plan on how to achieve them within their relationship.

Getting the Sex They Want

I then explore with them what they each want to get out of sex in a long-term relationship. As mentioned, we learn about sex when we are young and our bodies and relationships are young. What we were looking to get out of sex when learning about sex is likely going to be very different than what we are looking to get out it in an established partnership. I make sure clients are aware of this and provide the space to see if this changes what they realize they are actually looking for from sex right now. Once we learn what each wants from sex with each other, we then work toward that and do not waste our time on what they thought they should be wanting from sex or what they used to want from sex.

There are some sexual menu items meant for relationships that tend to work well with my gay male clients. These are items suggested by Treadway (2012): having them write letters recounting their favorite sexual experiences in the relationship or erotic fantasies; having light sexual play in places that will not allow things to lead to sex (in order to decrease the pressure of having to have sex); experimenting with their own masturbation experiences (to learn more about their own sexuality); and being satisfied with mediocre sex at times during a long-term relationship.

Working with Consensually Non-Monogamous (CNM) Relationships

As mentioned, a large portion of gay male couples are in some version of a CNM relationship. Monogamy being a concept that is very ingrained in

American culture, clinicians need to be especially careful about judgments and pathologizing of someone who is CNM. A clinician working with this community needs to be able to be mindful of their own biases and what they are bringing into the therapy room. I would recommend taking at least one class on CNM relationships and reading some of the books mentioned in the Resources section of this book. A significant portion of my clients in CNM relationships have had damaging experiences with previous therapists not properly prepared to work with these types of relationships.

I begin by assessing to what extent, if any, they have come out as CNM. If they have, I explore for any anxiety they have had around the life-long journey of coming out. Because society has such a strong bias toward monogamy being the only "right" way to be in a healthy relationship, coming out as anything that does not align with monogamy can potentially cause that individual a lot of stress, pain, and loss. Lavine (2010) found that for CNM relationships there is a tendency to only come out when a relevant situation arises. Pincus and Hiles (2017) speak to some of the main aspects considered by people deciding whether or not to come out as polyamorous: worry about morality clauses at places of employment allowing them to legally lose their jobs, how partners will deal with the disclosure, that children will get taken away because many see polyamorous relationships as just lots of sex happening all the time, and if, when, and how to tell their children about their identity. These stressors could easily contribute to sexual issues.

After understanding the coming-out experience, we begin work on what brought them into therapy. If what brings them in is that one or more partners wants to open up the relationship, I explore how each partner is feeling about this potential change. If one or more of the partners is unsure if their identity or relationship orientation is CNM, I suggest they complete Labriola's (2013) exercise of answering questions to get a sense of one's relationship orientation. We then review their results and explore how comfortable they would be practicing relationship dynamics corresponding to their results from the exercise. As a therapist, you need to be ready for each partner's current relationship style to be different from one another, even if they each started off as monogamous. I have had numerous clients realize that being CNM was a part of their identity and that they cannot be in a relationship that does not let them actualize that part of themselves. This does not mean that the other partner has to agree to be CNM or that the relationship needs to end (though sometimes ending the relationship is for the best). The outcome does not have to be that binary. A different dynamic to their relationship can be explored. This new dynamic may (or may not) involve them continuing some form of intimacy and/or sexual relationship.

If they are coming in for issues around jealousy, I validate that experiencing jealousy and being on the receiving end of jealousy can be extremely difficult. People in CNM relationships tend to have an increased shame when it comes to jealousy because they feel that only people in monogamous relationships get jealous, that somehow they should be above jealousy if they are in a CNM relationship. I normalize for these clients that jealousy often happens even in CNM relationships and let them know that they may not always feel jealous, or the same intensity of jealousy, because there are ways to work on jealousy.

While we do explore experiences for each partner around the jealousy, the bulk of the work is with the client who is feeling the jealousy. With them, I try to get an idea of what is behind the jealousy. It is common for jealousy to center around a perceived threat to an exclusive right or ownership of something (or someone); however, Rubinsky (2018) shows us that, for CNM individuals, their insecurity and jealousy tends to be less about fear of losing exclusivity and more about not getting their needs met. It is not uncommon for the jealousy to be around a partner not feeling they are getting to spend enough time with their partner or wishing that they themselves were having as good a time outside the relationship as their partner was. Once we find the cause or causes, then I work with them using Labriola's (2013) two-pronged approach to managing jealousy. One is a practical approach at figuring out the situations and behaviors that tend to trigger the jealousy and then figuring out ways to minimize or eliminate these. The other is to build tolerance of the feeling by gradually exposing oneself to the situations and behaviors that trigger them while using coping skills.

While healthy communication is crucial in any relationship, it is especially important in CNM relationships. Just think about the extra people, feelings, and events that are involved. My CNM clients will swear that a shared calendar is their best friend. When my clients come to me because of communication issues, I have found that, without fail (even if we have to go really slowly to get there), the Couples Institute's Developmental Model of Couple's Therapy's (created by Dr. Ellyn Bader) Initiator–Inquirer Process helps improve communication. The process includes the initiator bringing up an incident, sharing their experience of and feelings from that event, and the inquirer being curious to learn more about the initiator's experience, making sure to validate their partner, and helping the initiator realize why they were actually triggered around that incident. The case study below will provide an example of this communication tool.

Another extremely important part of a CNM relationship is a well-thought-out list of agreements. These are principles by which the partners agree to living in their relationship. Clients come to me because they want help in creating or changing their agreements. To give you an idea of what agreements are, here are some examples that I have found are popular (but not all encompassing) for gay men: "don't ask, don't tell" (which typically means each partner can have sex with others and the other partner does not want to know anything about it), no emotional connections (just physical sex), share if they plan not to be home for bed that night, fluid bonding (unprotected sex) is acceptable, no sex with ex-boyfriends or mutual friends, and only sex with others when they are together. I would recommend that any relationship, even those that are monogamous, have a collaborated-upon list of agreements, to make sure everyone understands what is going on in their relationship. Plenty of my monogamous couples have realized too late that they each had a different understanding of what monogamy actually meant for them.

When working on agreements we want to explore what realistically each client wants out of and can tolerate with an open relationship. For each, we will explore what they would want to be able to do outside the relationship, how much they want to know is happening outside the relationship, what would they like to keep just for the primary couple (if there is a primary couple), what kind of veto power a member of the primary couple gets, what are comfortable risk levels for sexually transmitted infections, would they feel better meeting metamours (partners of their partners), do they want a limit on how much time is spent with metamours or on hookup or dating sites, and how threatening are emotional connections with metamours.

We also need to make sure the agreements are as specific as possible and are setting up all partners for success. A break in an agreement is akin to infidelity and it will take a lot of work and time to rebuild the trust that was lost due to a transgression – if that is even a possibility. And secrecy and lies related to that break in an agreement will only intensify the hurt and trouble for the relationship. For that reason, I have my clients include in agreements a way partners can feel safe in sharing: if they did go against an agreement or if they pre-emptively want a change in an agreement. That is why I advocate with clients for them to be called agreements instead of rules because I want them to feel more fluid, as they can change over time depending on how the relationships evolve for each partner – as long as each partner agrees to the changes. We want to increase the chances that communication happens around a desire for a change and the agreement is not just disregarded. To help with this, I will often offer up and see how they feel about Addison & Clason's (2022) thinking that for those new to CNM relationships they may want "to make agreements that are time-limited, or that have 'sunset clauses' – commitments to check in and revisit how the agreements are working at specific future dates" (p. 309).

In order to increase the chances of success around CNM, if the family has children, then agreements will need to be made around aspects such as how much the children will know about the outside relationships and at what ages, how much to integrate metamours into the family, what metamours will be called/how they will be referred to by the family, and how nights spent out are explained. When figuring out in session how to disclose to a client's children, we tend to do a lot of work around wanting to make sure CNM relationships are not seen as something shameful to be hidden, while still appreciating the unfortunate reality that being completely out about it can cause confusion for and discrimination toward the child, and, as mentioned, real legal issues for the family.

For some guidance on setting up agreements, please visit this book's product page at www.routledge.com/9781032478715 and view Worksheet 6.

Sex While Being a Parent

When it comes to children in any relationship, there are some items to be taken into consideration around the adults' sex lives. I like to normalize for my gay male clients who are going to have or who already have children that sex is not likely going to be as much a priority or as easy to engage in. With children do come added stressors, less time and energy available for sex, and more situational barriers to sex, like having a child in your home or right across the hall from your bedroom. We work on ways to help the partners deal with these changes. For example, engaging in intimacy that may not take as much energy as sex used to take for them and exploring ways to feel comfortable and realistic about having a child in the house while having sex (a simple lock on the adults' bedroom door could make a big difference in putting one at ease).

I also bring up two of Perel's (2007) cautions around being a parent and sex: how starting one's own family could remind them of unhealthy or limited views of sex that they received from their own family of origin and watching out for a partner potentially getting all of their emotional and physical needs met from the children only. If dealing with the first, we will normalize what is occurring and look into ways to bring thinking into reality and remind them of their own values when it comes sex. For the second, we will also normalize the desire and ease to be completely consumed by the children and then find practical ways to limit what they are getting from the children and save some emotional and physical energy for their partner(s).

Most of us learned as children that love was good and lust was bad. For gay men, their lust was seen as especially bad because of the numerous reasons already discussed in this book. So when they are with a partner or partners for a while and move into a space of love and affection, they tend to feel that they can no longer lust after this person because that is incompatible with and bad when compared to love. If I believe this may be playing out for my clients, I explore their earliest memory of an experience that looking back was sexual, what was early messaging in the household around sex and desire versus love, and, if they see these ideas as opposites and with judgment, challenge their thinking and have them pay attention to their body to feel "that love and lust can and do interact" (Morin, 1995 p. 200).

Case Study

Leo is a 44-year-old able-bodied, white, gay, cisgender male, who uses he/him pronouns and Amir is a 27-year-old, Persian, able-bodied, gay, cisgender male, who uses he/him pronouns. They came to see me because they had recently opened up their relationship and were having difficulty navigating the parameters around the open relationship. This was causing them unhappiness, hurt, jealousy, and conflict. Even though they each wanted to be in an open relationship, they thought they may have to sacrifice this desire in order to save their relationship. Some of the major issues were related to Amir wanting to have sex more with guys on his own than Leo would allow. Leo was comfortable (and enjoyed) when they played together with others; however, when Amir wanted to play on his own, Leo would feel insecure, as if he was not enough for Amir. Leo did not like the heightened good mood Amir would get into when flirting with new guys on the hookup apps, wondering why Amir could not have that mood for Leo. Leo shared shame about having a "low" libido and therefore not being able to meet Amir's needs when it came to frequency of sex. And now, with Amir wanting to have sex with other guys on his own, Leo worried that he was not satisfying Amir enough when they were having sex. Leo spoke to imagining Amir wanted to have sex with other guys on his own so that he could have the kind of sex Amir really wanted, which was the type of sex portrayed in most porn.

Clinical Impressions

Leo and Amir were falling into the typical traps of most unhappy couples. They lacked knowledge of what healthy and pleasurable relationships and sex can look like. And they lacked skills to help them better communicate and be aware of, understand, and process feelings. Also, it seemed as if they had to revisit and talk through what their CNM relationship currently means for them and how their agreements will reflect this.

I felt happiness that they were coming to therapy to get guidance around their CNM relationship instead of just giving up on it. I was also happy because I got a sense that they were truly a fit, committed to each other, and could make their own and extended relationships work and be enjoyable.

Treatment

As was my usual practice, I wanted to talk about medical interventions. So I addressed the libido issue. I wanted to destigmatize having a lower libido than a partner, so helped them to see that Amir's libido was not better because it was higher than Leo's. They were just different. I also educated them on responsive versus spontaneous arousal and how arousal may occur if the person feels willing to try having sex. This resonated with both of them and opened up possibilities of increased frequency of sex. I also shared the study results of what leads to great sex, pointing out that nothing on the list speaks to spontaneous arousal. With that being said, I let Leo know that he could see a doctor about his libido if he chose to. I mentioned they would likely test testosterone levels; however, everyone has different levels and it is difficult to say where anyone's "should" be to maximize their libido. I also said that if he wanted to follow through on this, he would want to make sure that his testosterone levels were measured twice, at the same time of day for each test. I also made them each aware of the natural methods to increase testosterone (exercise, sleeping, and a balanced diet).

We then explored what each of them wanted from sex with each other and in a long-term relationship. Leo said that from sex with Amir he wanted connection and a rare space to be vulnerable with another man. For Amir, from sex with Leo he also wanted connection, as well as stimulation. We explored how they each could attain these goals, and there was a lot of over-lapping talk of touch, kissing, and holding. Again, none of this needed to be spontaneous or unplanned to still be enjoyable and meaningful.

One way we worked to get at understanding of what was behind the jealousy was to have Leo and Amir communicate using the Couples Institute's Developmental Model of Couple's Therapy's Initiator–Inquirer Process. Leo initiated by providing an example of a recent time when he experienced Amir as being head over heels for a guy he was talking to on Grindr. When Leo shared his version of the example, we used this as an opportunity to teach each of them that when they recount an event they are referring to their own experience of that event and we all experience the same events differently. I wanted to make sure that instead of thinking they were describing what had factually occurred in the past they realized it was their brain's interpretation and recall, and the brain is known for faulty recall and biases. This explanation of how the brain works helps each person become less attached to their version of an event and therefore more open to it having occurred a different way for someone else. It also makes it less likely that the receiver will become defensive upon hearing what is being shared. This is because it is not about what the partner did "wrong"; it is about how the initiator felt about what occurred. Amir, as the inquirer, asked Leo what it was like for him to experience Amir as head over heels for another guy. Leo explained feeling sad and hurt by this and not being able to fully concentrate for the rest of his day. After a while of sharing and asking questions, they were able to get to a place where they realized that, for Leo, as a child growing up in a household with six other siblings, there was daily competition to get their parents' attention and Leo "often lost", leading him to feel unsafe, sad, and as if he would not survive. Amir was able to show empathy and validation for the places Leo goes when he feels he might lose someone he loves and relies on. We used this insight to work on problem solving. We had Leo do self-talk around how he was no longer a child and, while he loved Amir, he did not need Amir the same way he needed his parents when a child, even though his brain/hard-wiring was telling him this was the case. Leo made use of Cognitive-Behavioral Therapy (CBT) sheets to work on the negative thinking and catastrophizing around the possibility of losing Amir.

To further work on the jealousy, we identified which situations and behaviors tended to trigger Leo. We took this information and worked on avoiding or changing these behaviors where Amir was open to doing so. And then figuring out how Leo could use his CBT skills and self-talk to gradually build up a tolerance of those situations and behaviors that continued to cause him discomfort. We also discussed that what he has with Amir is special and while Amir may experience new relationship energy with new guys, that was just a chemical change that they could work through with Leo making clear what his needs were when it came to Amir and new guys. This discussion of avoiding, changing, and needs led us to re-evaluate their agreements.

In terms of agreements, they each felt strongly about being each other's primary partner and if ever anyone would threaten this they would discuss how they, as the primary couple, would handle the development. Other agreements included no overnights, no more than two sex dates with others a week, prioritizing a date night for the two of them each week, a shared calendar so they knew when one of them was going to be out with a guy (this was especially helpful for Leo to plan around, so that he could build up his tolerance and also distract himself with plans), continuing to be on pre-exposure prophylaxis (PrEP) and fluid bond with other guys, allowing all sexual acts to be options with others, being able to see the same partner more than once, and having no romantic dates with other guys.

With the myths around sex brought into reality and his new set of skills, Leo was able to more easily enjoy the open relationship. And while he did not get to a place of being happy for Amir when Amir was with another man (compersion), he was able to much more easily tolerate these times, allowing them to both be able to experience their CNM identities.

I shared with Leo and Amir my being impressed that they were open to not letting monogamy just be a default for them and were willing to explore a CNM relationship, even when there were a few bumps along the way, while leaving space for the understanding that, just as monogamy is not for everyone, neither is a CNM relationship.

References

Addison, S.M., & Clason, N. (2022). "I will always come home to you": Affirmative therapy with clients practicing consensual non-monogamy. In R. Harvey, M.J. Murphy, J.J. Bigner, & J.L. Wetchler (Eds.), *Handbook of LGBTQ-Affirmative couple and family therapy*. New York, NY: Routledge.

Iasenza, S. (2020). *Transforming sexual narratives: A relational approach to sex therapy*. New York, NY: Routledge.

Kleinplatz, P.J., Menard, A.D., Paquet, M., Paradis, N. Campbell, M., Zuccarino, D., & Mehak, L. (2009). The components of optimal sexuality: A portrait of "great sex". *The Canadian Journal of Human Sexuality 18*(1–2), 1–13.

Labriola, K. (2013). *The jealousy workbook: Exercises and insights for managing open relationships*. Gardena, CA: Greenery Press.

Lavine, A.E. (2010). *What is the coming out experience of polyamorous individuals: an exploratory study: a project based upon an independent investigation*. Masters Thesis, Smith College, Northampton, MA.

Morin, J. (1995). *The erotic mind*. New York, NY: HarperCollins Publishers.

Peixoto, M.M. (2022). Affirming diversity and targeting pleasure: Sex therapy for gay male couples. In R. Harvey, M.J. Murphy, J.J. Bigner, & J.L. Wetchler (Eds.), *Handbook of LGBTQ-Affirmative couple and family therapy*. New York, NY: Routledge.

Perel, E. (2007). *Mating in captivity: Unlocking erotic intelligence*. New York, NY: HarperCollins.

Pincus, T. & Hiles, R. (2017). *It's called polyamory: Coming out about your nonmonogamous relationships*. Portland, OR: Thorntree Press.

Rubinsky, V. (2018). Bringing up the green-eyed monster: Conceptualizing and communicating jealousy with a partner who has other partners. *The Qualitative Report, 23*(6), 1441–1455.

Treadway, D. (2012). Heart's desire. In P.J. Kleinplatz (Ed.), *New directions in sex therapy*. New York, NY: Routledge.

Chapter 17

Safely Navigating Hookup Apps

Managing the Shame

When my gay male clients are using hookup apps, I speak to the value of having a platform where potentially one can find a sex or romantic partner or some feel a sense of community and freedom to be who they are. I do, however, also qualify these benefits.

To help normalize any trouble my clients are having with finding someone to hook up with, so that they do not feel that something is wrong with them, I make sure they know that people are going on the hookup apps for a wide range of reasons. Many of the users have no intention of meeting up with anyone for sex; however, they do make it seem as if they are on these apps to meet up for sex. This includes people who just want to chat via text, people who are looking to scam others out of money, those looking to just sell drugs, and those who are getting enough external validation from attention they get on the hookup apps (and so have no need to meet up in person). Once they wade through those profiles and are looking at the users who do intend to meet up for sex, they must then find someone who is a fit in terms of mutual attraction, what they are into sexually, and their availability for meeting up. They must then hope that when that meet-up time comes, they and the other person (or people) are still in the mood for sex.

When it comes to community and a space to be their authentic selves, I make sure we also discuss the blatant discrimination that occurs on the hookup apps. Based on my understanding of my client's intersectionality, I will mention what I am aware of in terms of stigma for that community or those communities and see if they have experienced this as well. If they have, we explore what they experience around this before opening a hookup app, while using it, and after putting it down. We also explore if actual sexual encounters from using the app have resulted in discrimination.

DOI: 10.4324/9781003386322-18

A lot of the gay men I see truly just want to find a boyfriend and I am a proponent of casting a wide net (especially since gay men do not have the same advantages in finding a romantic partner as their hetero-sexual counterparts) and I know that some long-term romantic rela-tionships have started through meeting on a hookup app. However, from what I have seen, this number is low and I ask clients, if they go down this road, to remind themselves that they are using an app focused on finding sex to find a boyfriend. I also warn them that while more formal dating apps do increase the chances of finding a boy-friend, when compared to hookup apps, they too can be used by peo-ple just looking for sex. I advise them that finding a fuller, more detailed profile on dating apps may increase the chances that the per-son is on the dating app looking for a boyfriend.

Pitfalls of Using the Apps

Some other issues that tend to come up are discomfort with the amount of and reasons for using hookup apps and the ramifications of being ghosted.

If a client feels that they are using these apps more than they would like, I will share with them the slot-machine analogy I mentioned in Chapter 9. They will often see how this applies and feel less shame about their usage levels. We will then explore what they are getting out of using hookup apps. Outside of hoping that they will find someone to have sex with, most of the time they will be going to these apps to get a hit of external validation. I explain to them how gay boys grew up not feeling good about themselves internally so only had external validation as a way to help make them feel good about themselves, and gay men are still wired for this. This education helps normalize their experience and reduces shame around wanting that external validation. We explore what kind of external validation they are getting from checking and being on the hookup apps. And then we look for ways to have them get that validation internally (through self-talk remind-ers of their worth or physical actions like self-hugging) and externally (through reaching out to friends or looking up reminders about how their friends see them). Sometimes it also helps to set up parameters around when they will use the apps and for how long and to turn off notifications on their phone from the apps. To help make this a success, we often explore the fear of missing out and try to bring thinking into reality around how much time spent on the hookup apps actually translates into getting the sex they want. To help clients be more intentional around hookup app usage, please visit this book's product page at www.routledge.com/9781032478715 and view Worksheet 7.

Ghosting is "the practice of suddenly ending a relationship by stopping all communication" (Gardiner, 2019, p. 166). Being ghosted has the ability to truly hurt someone, increase sadness, and/or send them into an anxious spiral of wondering what they, the client, did wrong. I validate what may come from being ghosted and then we work to bring their thinking into reality in terms of this behavior being about the other person and not having to do with whether or not the client was "good enough" or was not saying or doing the "right" things. What tends to help the client be able to embrace the reality that we tend to do things because of our own insecurities and learned coping skills (and not because of other people) is for them to see how they themselves are an examples of this. Also, I recommend they read *The Four Agreements* by Don Miguel Ruiz, to truly drive this point home. I also will use the Zimbardo experiment (mentioned in Chapter 9) to further illustrate how the chances for inappropriate and unkind behavior are increased on a platform of anonymity and remind them that not everyone on the app is even looking for sex, so ghosting is often utilized to get out of meeting up because that was never the intent.

I like to review with my clients who are using the hookup apps that a lot of people use these apps to make money. This usually happens through asking for small gifts (like a $10 gift card) to help them get through a troubling time; then the amounts requested get gradually larger. This is the old "foot in the door" technique. You feel like you could give larger sums because you already gave some money. Another scam is asking the user to invest money in something that is sure to pay back great dividends.

There is also sextortion. This is blackmail using sexually-related material they received from the user. If the blackmailer is able to get enough information from the user, they are able to find people the user is connected to (usually through social media) and threaten to share sexually explicit material of the user with the user's contacts unless a certain amount of money is paid. In a further effort to make sure they are as aware as possible on what is going on with the hookup apps, I review with them what I know about how drug offerings are made in profiles (as discussed in Chapter 9) so that they do not wind up in a situation that they were not expecting. I share this information not to scare my clients away from the hookup apps, but to make sure they are using them with their eyes wide open.

Case Study

Eric is a 42-year-old able-bodied, Vietnamese, gay, cisgender male, who uses he/him pronouns. He came to see me because he was convinced that he was "undatable" and wanted to figure out why. He shared how he had spent hours a day for the past few years on Grindr, Scruff, and Growlr (all popular hookup apps) and had yet to find someone for a long-term relationship.

Clinical Impressions

It seemed an education on how the hookup apps actually worked and the chances of meeting a boyfriend on them was extremely slim might help normalize his situation and get him to use other means to look for a long-term relationship.

I felt sadness for how Eric had been taken in by these alluring hookup apps, as well as frustration with Eric for relying on this one resource that had proven unsuccessful for years.

Treatment

We worked first to normalize that people are on hookup apps for many reasons. I shared with Eric that in my opinion, in descending order, people go on them to: 1) text in order to deal with boredom or to get an ego boost, 2) get aroused or get arousal satisfaction from texting or exchanging pics, 3) look for a sexual encounter, 4) just see who is in the area, 5) get money through scams, and 6) find a long-term relationship. Eric was able to share how he did think that not everyone on the app was looking for a boyfriend, but that he had likely, in his head, inflated the percentage of people who were. We explored why his brain might want to do that and Eric shared how hookup apps were so easy to use that he wanted them to eventually work. With this, we explored that these apps can be addictive and Eric did resonate with being taken in by the bells and whistles and how the hope of someone writing to him kept him constantly returning to the app. Like most gay men, Eric did grow up in a household where the idea of being gay was sinful, so he could not practice internal validation (since he saw himself on the inside as a bad person). However, as a human being, Eric needed some validation, so he wound up relying on getting it externally. This also resonated with Eric and helped him better understand his drive to seek approval from others. He shared how hookup apps could give him that external validation. I validated how thrilling it can be to get this for how one looks or comes across on a profile and we discussed the value of being able to also have some internal validation. I trusted Eric that he was getting positive feedback on the apps and I also wondered if he was experiencing any negative feedback, considering hookup apps in general and also that he was Asian. I explored this with Eric and he said that plenty of times he sees profiles that specifically mention "NO ASIANS" and that men expect that he will bottom and that he will not be very sexual. We had Eric pay attention to his body and what feelings these comments and beliefs had on him. He was able to notice a fire in his belly and get at the anger that was there. He had thought that he was successful at ignoring those comments or beliefs and just "moving on" but now he realized just how angry he was. I wanted him to recognize that a place that he turned to so often (hookup apps) did trigger anger for him, as well as plenty of invalidation. And that although he kept going back in the midst of all this negativity in hopes of getting those few incidents of reward (validation), that actually did not lead to his goal of finding a boyfriend. Through these realizations, Eric felt ready to limit his use of the apps and to put energy toward other ways to find a boyfriend.

We thought it would be valuable for Eric to start meeting people in person. More so than with hookup apps, this would allow him to be in an environment where the main reason for people engaging with each other was not initially sex, and for him to not just be ignored because he was assumed to be non-sexual. It would also allow him a distinct amount of time that he was at an event in person, rather than always having access to his phone and hence the hookup apps. We explored Meetup groups that were LGBTQ+-specific and involved an activity he liked. These included hiking, pot luck dinners, and brunches out. We also looked into meetings and groups at the New York City Gay & Lesbian Center, as they have a wide array of offerings and this location was easy enough for Eric to get to on a regular basis. Some of the towns around Eric had LGBTQ+ events in person, especially during June (Pride Month), which he wound up attending.

We also worked on Eric being more intentional in his use of the hookup apps. This meant setting timers to make him aware of how long he was spending on them, knowing why he was signing on, and making a note of how he was feeling before, during, and after use. We would explore these feelings in session to ensure that the apps were not doing more harm than good for Eric.

I used my sadness in session to help Eric be able to have some self-compassion around how he had been taken in by the app's tactics which influence many. I made sure to work through my frustration out of session, as I did not want to subject Eric to potentially feeling judged by his therapist.

Reference

Gardiner, L. (2019). Psychosexual history-taking in the 21st century: New terminology, new technology and new risks. *BJPsych Advances 25*, 166–176.

Chapter 18

Further Methods to Increase Pleasure

Increasing Pleasure As We Age

We will begin with the ways in which I work with gay men to have great sex later in life. As I mentioned previously, most of us stay stuck believing that we should be having sex the same way we did when we learned about sex, as teenagers and young adults. As our bodies age, we cannot do this. The great news is, we can have better sex as our bodies age. We can learn more about what actually stimulates us and brings us pleasure and practice that when having sex. Some other benefits of aging bodies for people with penises include more control over when you have sex (due to a lower libido and higher likelihood for responsive instead of spontaneous desire) and when you ejaculate (due to being less likely to ejaculate earlier than one would want).

While I like to point out the realistic advantages to sex as penis owners age, I also want to validate and normalize the challenges. Compared to when they were younger: their erections will take longer to achieve and will not be as firm, the refractory period (time after having an orgasm when the person is not sexually responsive) may be longer, the volume and intensity of ejaculatory decreases, and orgasms are less consistent. With this, we explore what the changing function of their genitals means to them and work to make sure they still see themselves as sexual beings.

To help their aging bodies be ready for sex, we discuss taking Vitamin D, staying hydrated, being intentional about their intake of carbohydrates and sugar, and looking to eat quality fats. Also, we will work on ways to sync their sex life with when they tend to have more energy and movement capabilities. We will also explore how medications may be affecting sex.

Since penis owners who are aged have less of an ability to be and stay erect, two toys that have specifically worked well to still provide stimulation to a penis that is not erect are Pulse and Cobra Libre. These toys are costly, at around $100 each, and are by no means necessary. If they are able, use of their hands is always a good option, with some barrier over the hands or penis that for them would increase the stimulation. Another area to focus on

DOI: 10.4324/9781003386322-19

is the prostate. Prostate massagers can be a lot of fun, but not an inexpensive, option for prostate owners. Look to Chapter 11 to ensure your client is using a safe and effective toy. If they are able, clients can use their finger to massage their prostate. They should wear a rubber glove (to avoid scratching) and make sure to use plenty of lube around the anus and on the finger they will insert into their anus. Then they would carefully insert that finger into the anus and feel around for a bump (the prostate) a few inches inside the rectum, and use the pad of their finger to press on or massage the bump. Soreness afterward is common and there may be some conditions (for example, hemorrhoids) that would warrant one not massaging the prostate. Please be aware that these toys and the focus on the prostate are by no means just pleasurable for the aged. Prostate orgasms have more pelvic floor contractions than a penile orgasm, so can feel more intense for anyone with a prostate. And if they still want to experience penetrating, there are hollow penis pullover strap-ons that they can place over their own penis. Some of these come with a vacuum to help with erection or a vibrator on top.

Some books to suggest to this community include *The Lives of LGBT Older Adults: Understanding Challenges and Resilience*, by Nancy Orel, *The Natural Testosterone Plan*, by Stephen Harrod Buhner, and *Naked At Our Age*, by Joan Price.

And for those living in elder care facilities, Simpson, Almack, and Walthery (2018) propose that these facilities focus more on the systems level by having a manager take the lead in getting out information on LGBT experiences and have face-to-face training on LGBT care. Leyerzapf, Visse, De Beer, and Abma (2018) speak to the importance of dialogue and narrative in residential care in order to allow for understanding of diversity around sexual orientation and gender and "safety, respect, and personal and social recognition" (p. 370).

Increasing Pleasure for Transgender, Non-Binary, and/or Queer (TGNBQ) Individuals

With my TGNBQ gay clients, I want to first validate some of the issues that tend to be unique to this population that get in the way of increased sexual pleasure. "TGNBQ people are eroticized and exoticized – except of course when they are viewed as non-sexual and incapable of human intimacy" (Lev & Sennott, 2022, p. 149). So, I like to acknowledge that this treatment and misconception could likely be where most of my TGNBQ gay clients are starting from when it comes to sex. I also validate that their journey to figuring out what brings them pleasure in sex, even including what types of partners they prefer, is often wrapped up in them first figuring out their gender identity (Lev & Sennott, 2022).

If they speak of trouble getting needs or wants met during sex, I also normalize this by sharing that, when compared to cisgender MSM (men who have sex with men), trans MSM are less likely to report having their sexual needs met, specifically around sex being as safe as they would like it to be and saying no to sex that they do not want (Appenroth et al., 2022). Hickson et al. (2020) found that it was especially difficult for trans men to say no to unwanted sex. When I explore the reasons behind this with my clients, often we realize they are feeling anxiety in sexual situations because they are worried about not having the body that a partner would want them to have. This anxiety and negative view of their own body gets in the way of them being present enough to have the capacity to say no and feeling as if they have the right to say no. To combat this, we work on breathing exercises and other ways to get them out of survival mode when in sexual situations and bringing their thinking into reality so that they are able to have a better relationship to their body and needs. To accomplish the latter, I work to support "clients in developing language to identify their sexual desires" and to ensure that:

> Therapy is geared not at accepting the limits of the anatomical body, but rather at expanding the possibilities of emerging identity, where one's physicality does not necessarily represent one's actual identity. Over time, the dysphoria can evaporate and transform into gender congruence.
>
> (Lev & Sennott, 2012, p. 330)

Sometimes clients have trouble celebrating and being comfortable with their bodies during sex because of the societal messaging that sex needs to focus on genitalia and that genitalia needs to look and experience sensation in just one way. To help get away from genitalia as the major focus of sex, I use Fielding's (2021) guidance on coming into compassionate relationship:

> Coming into compassionate relationship explodes the tired dichotomies and modes of binary thinking. It gives the lie to the idea that sex has to look or feel a certain way, involve particular acts, or even involve genitals. Steeped in a stance of ethical curiosity, therapy with trans and non-binary folx can promote a play space within the therapeutic container to imaginally explore and re-constitute how desire and eroticism can show up in new ways in the body…
>
> (p. 78)

To accomplish this we work on sexual menus and lots of exploring of the body during masturbation to expand their knowledge around what masturbation can look like and what can feel good sensually.

This does not mean that all transgender and non-binary individuals should not or do not want to also focus on and enjoy their genitalia. However, do not assume you know what clients call their genitalia. Some of my clients will call what is commonly known as a clitoris (which will be enlarged if they have taken testosterone to affirm their identity) their penis or cock. They will also call what is commonly known as the vulva their bonus, extra, or front hole or man cunt. As a therapist trying to navigate talk of genitalia without assuming we know what a client calls their parts, Fielding (2021) has provided some alternatives to commonly used labels:

- External genitalia (instead of vulva)
- Erectile tissue (instead of clitoris or penis)
- Glans (instead of clitoris or head of penis)
- Lateral folds (instead of labia)
- Canal, opening, or introitus (instead of vagina)
- Gonads (instead of ovaries or testes)
- Skin or pouch covering gonads (instead of scrotum)

(pp. 166–167)

Some TGNBQ clients will have undergone a form of medical intervention to help them with affirmation. These procedures have the capability to directly affect sex. "Medical and surgical treatments can impact physiology as well as psychology, and have predictable effects, both positive and negative on sexual satisfaction" (Lev & Sennott, 2022, p. 159). When looking at individuals assigned female at birth who have affirmed to male, Costantino et al. (2013) found that:

> After 1 year of testosterone administration subjects experienced an improvement in general sexual function compared with baseline. In particular, frequency of masturbation, sexual desire, arousal, and sexual fantasies were the most affected parameters. In the postsurgery questionnaires, sexual parameters returned to baseline in most of the subjects, remaining increased for only about 25%. Total testosterone levels were positively associated only with frequency of sexual intercourse.
>
> (p. 330)

Wierckx et al. (2014) found that 71% of trans men experienced higher arousal after surgery, 17% experienced no change at all, and 12% experienced a decrease and no major differences were shown to be based on sexual orientation. After surgery, individuals have to learn how to interact with and get pleasure from those parts where the surgery was performed. This is where an intervention of "coming into (com)passion relationship with the embodied sexual self can be especially helpful" (Fielding, 2021, p. 155). Fielding (2021) suggests utilizing what the client is going through post-surgery by working with them to deeply tap into what they are fully experiencing in their bodies or have them access their wants around "how they want a surgically-facilitated body part to be interacted with and felt" (p. 155).

There may also be grief that happens post-surgery, as there is at least some loss that is occurring. "We can help our clients mourn what has changed, celebrate what was so profoundly anticipated, and resist cultural scripts of function and performance to embrace how pleasure shows up for them" (Fielding, 2021, p. 155).

Any therapist working with TGNBQ clients must take a closer look at their own identity and communicate what they are comfortable sharing about their own gender, in order to help build connection with an individual who has likely struggled around their identity (Fielding, 2021). And if a therapist is having clinical trouble with sessions, they would do best to get education and supervision around these issues, instead of burdening the client with the role of educator, as "this can feel re-traumatizing for some TGNBQ people" (Lev & Sennott, 2022, p. 163). This does not mean the therapist does not ask any questions, as they need to; however, they need to be more intentional about exploring their own entitlement when it comes to questions they just automatically feel they have the right to ask TGNBQ clients. Fielding (2021) suggests that before asking questions to clients, therapists ask themselves why they are asking that question, what assumptions they are bringing to this particular interaction, and who actually needs to educate the clinician on the material the client is presenting.

And, finally, in order to help TGNBQ individuals get some stimulating material to help them learn more about their bodies and sensual pleasure, I suggest Fielding's (2021) recommendations: publications https://transsexzine.com and https://originalplumbing.bigcartel.com and the film site https://www.aortafilms.com.

Increasing Pleasure for Persons with Disabilities and/ or Chronic Illness

The work of truly getting an individual to connect with their body is also crucial for many people with disabilities and chronic illness and pain. Breathing exercises that connect to the body, actual self-touring of the body, and Viniyoga (yoga that is customized for each practitioner) can be effective ways to help this population connect to and have their bodies feel sexual (Kaufman, Silverberg, & Odette, 2007). Other tips from Kaufman, Silverberg, and Odette (2007) to enhance pleasure during sex include:

- Talk about the effects of pain during sex, rather than trying to describe the pain itself.
- Agree that the person with the pain or limitation knows best about what is ok during sex.

- Understand that basic hierarchy of needs may, understandably and realistically, get in the way of prioritizing sex, and still managing energy reserves and time for sex and taking breaks during sex.
- Learn how to communicate around sex with a partner or partners without using words, in order to deal with physical limitations around speech or lack of privacy.
- Understand that masturbation can take on so many forms that do not involve touching the body, from fantasizing to just watching porn.
- Asking what being aroused and sexual pleasure means for them and how they know they are ready to end having sex.
- To find sexual partners: get involved in a cause they care about, online and apps, hire a sex worker (letting them know your disability and what you want, having a safety plan during the encounter, and getting a referral when possible), or hire a sexual surrogate.
- Figure out how to negotiate with an attendant around help with masturbation or sex with others (if they feel safe or comfortable doing so).

A sex pillow (a cushion that allows for easier angling of the body to assist with sexual positions) is useful for anyone having sex and tends to be especially useful during sex for persons with disabilities and/or chronic pain. They come in various sizes, shapes, and prices, so the client would need to find the one that makes the most sense for what they are trying to achieve when having sex.

The Likely Pleasure Points

While I do encourage clients to make use of any body part as a sensual body part and never assume that a body part needs to be used in a certain way, there are some body parts that tend to be more sensitive and help the owner receive pleasure (often due to erectile tissue being present or a lot of nerve endings). Here are most of them for cisgender and TGNBQ individuals:

- Perineum – the space between the scrotum or vulva and anus
- Root of the penis
- Pubic bone – next to the clitoris
- Head of the penis
- Hood of the clitoris
- Labia
- Urethral sponge – the fatty tissue around the urethra, near the top of the vaginal canal
- Meatus – the hole at the end of the urethra

- Anus
- Prostate
- Frenulum – the small skin on the underside of the penis head
- Nipples

When helping clients choose sex toys that will bring them pleasure, you want to know if they have used any in the past and, if they have, what did they like and dislike about it, and what they are looking to get out of a new toy. You also want to explore what types of toys they are able to handle and work with based on their abilities (for example, someone may need a hands-free toy or something with a harness), the size and power they are looking for, and how much money they are comfortable spending. And I often suggest to clients that, like most things, a toy takes some getting used to, so they will want to use it a few times (if not causing them any harm or pain) before deciding whether or not it can enhance their pleasure.

Kink/Bondage, Discipline/Domination, Sadism/ Submission, and Masochism (BDSM) as an Option

When helping clients choose how they want to have sex, I often will explore kink/BDSM with them as a world full of options for them to explore. According to Goerlich (2021):

Kink has two definitions. First, kink is simply sexual practices that go beyond what is considered conventional as a means of heightening the intimacy between sexual partners – heightening intimacy being the key component. Not all kink play results in intercourse…The second definition of kink is a bit more literal. It's a sharp twist or curve in something that is otherwise straight, such as a line or a road.

(p. 5)

While Rehor (2015) explains that:

Someone who is kinky engages in unconventional sensual, erotic, and sexual behavior including BDSM-related behaviors (physical and psychological stimuli including bondage, discipline, dominance, submission, sadism and masochism), exhibitionistic behaviors (arousal by being observed by others), voyeuristic behaviors (arousal by observing others), fetishistic behaviors (arousal by objects), and others.

(p. 826)

Kink/BDSM play will often (but not always) involve role play and/or power dynamics, with someone in a dominant role engaging with someone in a submissive role. Each person in those roles gets satisfaction from being dominant or submissive and those who are submissive actually are in a powerful position, as they have ultimate say in terms of what can and cannot occur during a scene. Negotiating agreements of what will happen during and after play, consent, connection, transparency, mutual regard, inclusion, and safety (Goerlich, 2021) are very important and necessary aspects of kink/BDSM, contributing to it having the potential to be pleasurable, healthy, and healing. These are some of the reasons I feel so many people, especially gay men, can benefit from being exposed to kink/BDSM.

Hebert and Weaver (2015) found that for kinksters BDSM play improved their lives, provided a means for deep self-exploration, and allowed them to freely experience different parts of themselves, which fluctuated based on their partner's and their own needs at the time. They also found that some felt that BDSM allowed them to be more authentic to their true selves, more so than the roles they played in everyday life.

I find it helpful to give gay men some alternatives to the sex that they are already likely familiar with and normalize these sexual practices that are not commonplace but may be exactly what they need to experience for ultimate pleasure and stimulation during sex. I educate them on the key components of kink (negotiation, consent, play, aftercare, and debriefing) and make them aware of the cautionary signs that tell them they are not engaging in kink/BDSM. Some examples of these include someone either not using or guilting someone for using safe words, asking a partner to consent to something new during a scene or while intoxicated, continuing behavior outside of scenes if that was not part of the negotiation, and not taking health issues into consideration. If my clients want to explore kink/BDSM I refer them to local classes, online classes (KinkAcademy.com), and literature (*The Ultimate Guide to Kink: BDSM. RolePlay and the Erotic Edge* by Tristan Taormino [2012], *Different Loving Too: Real People, Real Lives, Real BDSM* by Gloria G. Brame [2015], and *Playing Well with Others: Your Field Guide to Discovering, Navigating and Exploring Kink, Leather and BDSM Communities* by Lee Harrington [2013]).

For clinicians working with kink/BDSM clients, I recommend *The Leather Couch: Clinical Practice with Kinky Clients* by Stefani Goerlich (2021), Kinkawareprofessionals.com, and Kinkguidelines.com.

Case Study

Ter is a 24-year-old able-bodied, white, gay, transgender male, who uses he/him pronouns. He came to see me because he had recently realized his sexual orientation as gay and was not having great success when having sex with men. Ter shared often feeling objectified during sex and that his lack of experience with sex with men meant that he had to just follow a partner's lead (having sex the partner wanted). He knew he wanted more stimulation and pleasure than letting a partner decide all that would happen, but he was worried about rejection. Ter shared that his two main reasons for worrying about rejection were: 1) if he was a fetish (object), then the partner could just find another FTM (a person who transitions/affirms their identity from being assigned female at birth to male) person to have sex with next time and 2) if he was not a fetish, then the guy was doing Ter a "favor" by having sex with him. With either scenario that Ter made up in his mind, he was coming into sexual encounters at a disadvantage. These lack of pleasurable experiences during sex were leaving Ter sad and hopeless, and even questioning his sexual identity.

Clinical Impressions

Ter was picking up on real messaging that is out there related to transgender men and we could work to help him realize that not all men felt that way. And he could use therapy as a safe space to do some real soul searching around what now brought him pleasure.

I felt sadness that Ter's entry into sex with men was not proving so satisfying and happiness that he sought out therapy and this would be a space that he could figure out what brought him pleasure.

Treatment

We began with me validating what Ter was sharing in terms of how some guys may be treating and seeing him and the disadvantage one may feel with inexperience. Early on we used some Cognitive-Behavioral Therapy (CBT) work to help him change his 'all or nothing' thinking and mind reading around what all men were thinking about him. We also discussed how even when men have multiple years of sexual experience that does not mean they know what they are doing or have the magic code to what is pleasurable. Ter was able to take in how with sex most men are flying by the seat of their pants and he need not enter a sexual situation feeling that the partner knows best. He was also able to realize that the only person that could figure out what was best for Ter when it came to sex was Ter himself. He would have to learn what those things were and communicate them to others.

To begin to figure out what he wanted from sex, I asked whether or not his sexual identity journey had been wrapped up in his gender identity journey. Ter shared that as far back as he was able to remember, he was male and when it came to sexual orientation he was a straight, as he was romantically and sexually attracted to women. However, once he started his hormone therapy, he realized that he actually was gay – he felt romantic and sexual attraction to mostly men. Ter already knew that becoming aware of a different sexual orientation happened for some transgender men. He felt relieved that he did not have a girlfriend at the time he was making this realization, so he would not have to worry about dealing with trying to manage and go through a breakup. It was helpful for me to understand that even the idea of sex with men was a new concept for Ter.

Ter was a big sci-fi fan, so I asked him to escape into a world where all preconceived notions of what men wanted to do and get out of sex were erased and we were evolved beings that could get pleasure from any part of our bodies and minds. After he created this world, I asked that he think about what he would want to get out of and experience from sex in that world. Ter did not stray too far away from what was typical when it came to sex, and I did not see a reason to push him to do so. He wanted stimulation to his now larger dick through oral sex and hand play. He wanted to suck cock, rim (perform oral sex on the anus), and find out what it felt like to be rimmed. He also wanted to kiss confidently – feeling like he had the "authority" to look into someone's eyes and hold the back of their head while kissing. With his increased realistic thinking about how he can be seen and what can happen during sex, Ter felt ready to take a risk and experiment with letting guys know beforehand what he was looking for from sex, get consent, and follow through with these activities. As he did so, he still met some guys that were objectifying him; however, he learned to not engage with these men, leave that situation, and not see that situation as indicative of how all men saw or would see him. Getting so much pleasure out of the sexual activities he described helped him to feel more whole and more assured in his identity as a gay man.

I shared my happiness with Ter to validate what may come out of choosing therapy as a resource. I also shared my sadness with Ter so that he could potentially get a sense that he deserved more out of sex and then worked to show him that my sadness did not contain hopelessness, as I knew he could figure this out.

References

Appenroth, M.N., Koppe, U., Hickson, F., Schink, S., Hahne, A., Schmidt, A.J., Weatherburn, P., & Marcus, U. (2022). Sexual happiness and satisfaction with sexual safety among German trans men who have sex with men: results from EMIS-2017. *Journal of the International AIDS Society* 25(S5), 11–18.

Costantino, A., Cerpolini, S., Alvisi, S., Morselli, P.G., Venturoli, S., & Meriggiola, M.C. (2013). A prospective study on sexual function and mood in female-to-male transsexuals during testosterone administration and after sex reassignment surgery. *Journal of Sex and Marital Therapy 39*, 321–335.

Fielding, L. (2021). *Trans sex: Clinical approaches to trans sexualities and erotic embodiments*. New York, NY: Routledge.

Goerlich, S. (2021). *The Leather Couch: Clinical Practice with Kinky Clients*. New York, NY: Routledge.

Hebert, A. & Weaver, A. (2015). Perks, problems, and the people who play: A qualitative exploration of dominant and submissive BDSM roles. *The Canadian Journal of Human Sexuality 24*(1), 49–62.

Hickson, F., Appenroth, M., Koppe, U., Schmidt, A.J., Reid, D., & Weatherburn, P. (2020). Sexual and mental health inequalities across gender identity and sex-assigned-at-birth among men-who-have-sex-with-men in Europe: Findings from EMIS-2017. *International Journal of Environmental Research and Public Health* 17, 7379–7399.

Kaufman, M, Silverberg, C., & Odette, F. (2007). *The ultimate guide to sex and disability: For all of us who live with disabilities, chronic pain, and illness*. San Francisco, CA: Cleis Press, Inc.

Lev, A.I. & Sennott, S.L. (2012). Understanding gender nonconformity and transgender identity: A sex-positive approach. In P.J. Kleinplatz (Ed.), *New directions in sex therapy*. New York, NY: Routledge.

Lev, A.I. & Sennott, S.L., (2022). Sexuality and desire landscapes in transgender, nonbinary, and genderqueer relationships. In R. Harvey, M.J. Murphy, J.J. Bigner, & J.L. Wetchler (Eds.), *Handbook of LGBTQ-Affirmative couple and family therapy*. New York, NY: Routledge.

Leyerzapf, H., Visse, M., De Beer, A. and Abma, T.A. (2018). Gay-friendly elderly care: creating space for sexual diversity in residential care by challenging the hetero norm. *Aging & Society*, *38*, 352–377.

Rehor, J.E. (2015). Sensual, erotic and sexual behaviors of women from the "kink" community. *Archive of Sexual Behavior* 44, 825–836.

Simpson, P., Almack, K., & Walthery, P. (2018). 'We treat them all the same': the attitudes, knowledge and practices of staff concerning old/er lesbian, gay, bisexual and trans residents in care homes. *Aging & Society*, *38*, 869–899.

Wierckx, K.M.D., Elaut, E, Van Hoorde, B., Heylens, G., De Cuypere, G., Monstrey, S., Weyers, S., Hoebeke, P., & T'Sjoen, G. (2014). Sexual desire in trans persons: Associations with sex reassignment treatment. *The Journal of Sexual Medicine*, *11*, 107–118.

Resources

Therapy

If your client needs to find another therapist, I suggest referring them to directories that have queer knowledgeable and affirming therapists. I would also advise that your clients not immediately trust a therapist profile that says they are LGBTQ+ affirming or knowledgeable. It is easy for a clinician to check a box that relates to working with LGBTQ+ clients and truly feel they have the capability to work with this population, even if they really do not. If the written portion of the therapist's profile does not give some detailed explanation of their work with the LGBTQ+ community, I tell clients to stay away from those clinicians. Once your client has found some therapists that seem like they may be a fit, I would recommend they have free brief consultations with those potential clinicians to get a sense of their work with LGBTQ+ clients. Also, I make sure my clients know that once they have begun therapy, if they find that person is not actually working for them, that they need to advocate for themselves with that therapist, and that this may mean ultimately finding a new therapist.

In order to increase the chances that the therapist will be queer knowledgeable and affirming, I would recommend using the directories below. Using these directories will not guarantee that the therapist is as queer-informed as a client might need, so they will still want to do their homework and get a sense of the clinician's fit for them.

American Association of Sexuality Educators, Counselors, and Therapists (AASECT)
aasect.org/referral-directory
The Association of LGBTQ+ Psychiatrists
aglp.memberclicks.net/aglp-referral
FindTreatment.gov (Under their Special Programs there is a search filter for LGBTQ+)
GLBT National Help Center
glbtnearme.org
Gaylesta
directory.gaylesta.org/find-a-therapist/?user=find-a-therapist
The Kink and Polyamory Aware Professionals Directory (KAP)

kapprofessionals.org
National Queer and Trans Therapists of Color Network
nqttcn.com/en
Open Path Psychotherapy Collective
openpathcollective.org (lower-cost psychotherapy with LGBTQ+ option under their
    Specialties section)
Poly Friendly Professionals
polyfriendly.org/categories/psychotherapists-licensed-or-registered
Pride Counseling
pridecounseling.com
PsychologyToday.com (multiple search filters, including LGBTQ+ and sex therapy)
PFLAG
pflag.org/findachapter (free groups for LGBTQ+ individuals and their families and
    allies)
World Professional Association for Transgender Health.
wpath.org/provider/search

Asexuality

Book

The Invisible Orientation: An Introduction to Asexuality - Julie Sondra Decker

Other

AOK – podcast
Asexuality.org
@asexuallove and @asexual.aesthetic – Instagram
Life in a Sex Vacuum – YouTube

Consensual Non-Monogamy

Books

The Anxious Person's Guide to Non-Monogamy – Lola Phoenix
*Designer Relationships: A Guide to Happy Monogamy, Positive Polyamory, and Opti-
    mistic Open Relationships* – Mark A. Michaels & Patricia Johnson
*The Ethical Slut: A Practical Guide to Polyamory, Open Relationships, & Other Ad-
    ventures* - Janet W. Hardy & Dossie Easton
It's Called Polyamory: Coming Out About Your Nonmonogamous Relationships – Ta-
    mara Pincus & Rebecca Hiles
The Jealousy Workbook – Kathy Labriola
Love In Abundance: A Counselor's Advice on Open Relationships - Kathy Labriola
*Love's Not Colorblind: Race and Representation in Polyamorous and Other Alterna-
    tive Communities* - Kevin A. Patterson

More than Two: A Practical Guide to Ethical Polyamory – Franklin Veaux & Eve Rickert

Opening Up: A Guide to Creating and Sustaining Open Relationships – Tristan Taormino

The Polyamorists Next Door – Elisabeth Sheff

Polysecure: Attachment, Trauma, and Consensual Nonmonogamy – Jessica Fern

Power Circuits: Polyamory in a Power Dynamic – Raven Kaldera

Sex At Dawn: How We Mate, Why We Stray, and What It Means for Modern Relationships - Christopher Ryan & Cacilda Jetha

Sites

Lovemore.com
Morethantwo.com
ncsfreedom.org
polyamory.org
Polymatchmaker.com
OKCupid.com
Facebook Group: OLNY (Open Love New York)
Thebodysacred.com

Podcast

Multiamory

KINK/Bondage, Discipline/Domination, Sadism/ Submission, and Masochism (BDSM)

Books

Different Loving Too: Real People, Real Lives, Real BDSM – Gloria G. Brame

Playing Well with Others: Your Field Guide to Discovering, Exploring and Navigating the Kink, Leather and BDSM Communities – Lee Harrington & Mollena Williams

Sacred Kink: The Eightfold Paths of BDSM and Beyond – Lee Harrington

SM 101: A Realistic Introduction – Jay Wiseman

The Ultimate Guide to Kink: BDSM, Role Play and the Erotic Edge – Tristan Taormino

Sites

bdsm-checklist.pdffiller.com

The Eulenspiegel Society (TES) (classes, workshops and events in the NY tri-state area) - tes.org

Fet Life (like Facebook for the kink/BDSM community) fetlife.com

KinkAcademy.com (free and paid videos on BDSM instruction)
The National Coalition for Sexual Freedom
ncsfreedom.org

Video

Morgan Thorne on Kink and Chronic Pain
youtube.com/watch?v=vQjERbp8Rg8

Religion

United Methodists for LGBTQIA People and Our Allies
umaffirm.org
Dignity USA: Celebrating the wholeness and holiness of LGBTQIA+ Catholics
dignityusa.org
Friends for Lesbian, Gay, Bisexual, Transgender, and Queer Concerns (North American Quaker Faith Community)
flgbtqc.org
Gay and Lesbian Vaishnava Association
galva108.org
Gay, Lesbian and Affirming Disciples Alliance, Inc.
gladalliance.org
Metropolitan Community Churches
mccchurch.org
United Church of Christ
openandaffirming.org
Lutherans for Full Participation
reconcilingworks.org
The World Congress of GLBT Jews
glbtjews.org

Sex

Sex – ADHD

Book

ADHD After Dark – Ari Tuckman

Videos

Is ADHD Affecting Your Sex Life? https://www.youtube.com/watch?v=Jdk9pONHEEM
ADHD Aha! Sex, intimacy, and ADHD https://www.youtube.com/watch?v=xL_3kJQHlyk

The Impact of ADHD on Sex & Relationships https://www.youtube.com/watch?v=CJks96Sjvv4

ADHD After Dark: How to Improve Your Sex Life https://www.youtube.com/watch?v=m8QNRpN4nY8

Podcast

Struggle Care Episode 36: ADHD & Sex with Catie Osborn

Sex – Aged Populations

Books

The Lives of LGBT Older Adults: Understanding Challenges and Resilience – Nancy Orel

Naked at Our Age: Talking Out Loud About Senior Sex – Joan Price

The Natural Testosterone Plan: For Sexual Health and Energy – Stephen Harrod Buhner

Ultimate Guide to Sex & Disability: For All of Us Who Live with Disabilities, Chronic Pain, and Illness – Miriam Kaufman

Sex – General

Books

Anal Pleasure & Health – Jack Morin

Arousal: The Secret Logic of Sexual Fantasies – Michael J. Bader

Come As You Are: The Surprising New Science that Will Transform Your Sex Life – Emily Nagoski

The Erotic Mind: Unlocking the Inner Sources of Passion and Fulfillment – Jack Morin

Erotic Orientation: Helping Couples and Individuals Understand Their Sexual Lives – Joe Kort

Mating in Captivity: Unlocking Erotic Intelligence – Esther Perel

Sexual Intelligence: What We Really Want from Sex and How to Get It – Marty Klein

Treating Out of Control Sexual Behavior: Rethinking Sex Addiction – Douglas Braun-Harvey and Michael A. Vigorito

Urban Tantra, Second Edition: Sacred Sex for the Twenty-First Century – Barbara Carrellas

Why Good Sex Matters: Understanding the Neuroscience of Pleasure for a Smarter, Happier, and More Purpose-Filled Life – Nan Wise

Sites

bodyelectric.org (offers expertly guided educational experiences grounded in the erotic and its integration with the sacred, to foster transformative personal and communal healing)

Mojoupgrade.com (a discrete way to figure out what you and your partner(s) are into sexually)

Ohjoysextoy.com

Scarleteen (for teens and young adults)

Sex – Persons with Disability & Chronic Illness and Pain

Books

The Illustrated Guide to Better Sex for People With Chronic Pain – Robert W. Rothrock, G. D'Amore, Jonathan Belt

A Quick & Easy Guide to Sex & Disability (Quick & Easy Guides) – A. Andrews

Sex and Disability – Robert McRuer

Sex-Interrupted: Igniting Intimacy While Living With Illness or Disability – Iris Zink

Sex and Relationships Education for Young People and Adults with Intellectual Disabilities and Autism – Jay Burns

Sexuality and Intellectual Disabilities: A Guide for Professionals – Andrew Maxwell Triska

Ultimate Guide to Sex & Disability: For All of Us Who Live with Disabilities, Chronic Pain, and Illness – Miriam Kaufman

What Is Sex?: A Guide for People With Autism, Special Educational Needs and Disabilities (Healthy Loving, Healthy Living) – Kate E. Reynolds

Sites

bentvoices.org (queer crip culture)

chronicbabe101.com (to help feel more savvy, sexy, and confident as you navigate your chronic illness journey)

comeasyouare.com/blogs/sex-information/sex-and-disability (guide on adapting sex toys)

msmorganthorne.com (BDSM education from a professional dominant, who has chronic pain and a disability)

Toy sites that take into account disability: goodvibes.com, mypleasure.com, stockroom.com, intimaterider.com

Videos

Sin Invalid Performances

youtube.com/watch?v=K3eZp2DdlLA

youtube.com/watch?v=TkSG5NKRALs

youtube.com/watch?v=tj9EeQsh4Lk

Sex – Persons with External Genitalia/Vulvas

Books

Becoming Cliterate: Why Orgasm Equality Matters – And How to Get It – Laurie Mint

Come As You Are: The Surprising New Science that Will Transform Your Sex Life – Emily Nagoski

Completely Overcome Vaginismus – Lisa & Mark Carter
Reclaiming Your Sexual Self: How You Can Bring Desire Back Into Your Life – Kathryn Hall
Sex for One: The Joy of Selfloving – Betty Dodson

Sites

Debunkingdesire.com
HappyDownThere.ca
Meetrosy.com (help with sexual issues)
OMGYes.com (site on orgasm)
Vulvagallery.com & labialibrary.au
Vaginismus.com

Sex – Persons with Erectile Tissue/Penises

Book

The New Male Sexuality: The Truth About Men, Sex, and Pleasure – Bernie Zilbergeld

Online

drsusieg.com. (information on pelvic and sexual health)
YouTube Video: Private Dicks (video of real naked men being vulnerable and helping to normalize different types of bodies)
youtube.com/watch?v=3-PgyZRbkrQ

Sex – Persons with Prostates

Book

Ultimate Guide to Prostate Pleasure: Erotic Exploration for Men and Their Partners – Charlie Glickman

Sex – Transgender, Non-Binary, and/or Queer (TGNBQ)

Books

Queer Sex: A Trans and Non-Binary Guide to Intimacy, Pleasure and Relationships – Juno Roche
Trans/Love: Radical Sex, Love & Relationships Beyond the Gender Binary – Morty Diamond

Substance Issues

Bicycle Health (LGBGTQ+ Summary and AA & NA Meetings)
bicyclehealth.com/blog/substance-use-disorder-lgbtq-community

Substance Issues – LGBTQ+ Residential Programs

inspirerecovery.com
mainlinehealth.org/specialties/mirmont-lgbtq
pride-institute.com
therefuge-ahealingplace.com

Trauma

Books

The Body Keeps the Score: Brain, Mind, and Body in the Healing of Trauma – Bessel van der Kolk
Heal the Body, Heal the Mind: A Somatic Approach to Moving Beyond Trauma – Susanne Babbel
Healing Sexual Trauma – Staci Haines
Queering Sexual Violence – Radical Voices from Within the Anti-Violence Movement – Jennifer Patterson
Violence and Abuse in the Lives of People With Disabilities: The End of Silent Acceptance? – Dick Sobsey
Waking the Tiger: Healing Trauma – Peter A. Levine
Written in the Body: Letters from Trans and Non-Binary Survivors of Sexual Assault and Domestic Violence – Bean

Clinicians

Books

The Body Keeps the Score: Brain, Mind, and Body in the Healing of Trauma – Bessel van der Kolk
Come As You Are: The Surprising New Science that Will Transform Your Sex Life – Emily Nagoski
Compulsive Sexual Behaviors: A Psycho-Sexual Treatment Guide for Clinicians – Silva Neves
Couple Therapy with Gay Men – David E. Greenan and Gil Tunnell
Handbook of LGBTQ-Affirmative Couple and Family Therapy – Rebecca Harvey, Megan J. Murphy, Jerry J. Bigner, & Joseph L. Wetchler (Editors)
The Invisible Orientation: An Introduction to Asexuality – Julie Sondra Decker
LGBTQ Clients in Therapy: Clinical Issues and Treatment Strategies – Joe Kort
The Leather Couch: Clinical Practice with Kinky Clients – Stefani Goerlich

The Modern Clinician's Guide to Working with LGBTQ+ Clients: The Inclusive Psychotherapist – Margaret Nichols

More than Two: A Practical Guide to Ethical Polyamory – Franklin Veaux and Eve Rickert

Naked at Our Age: Talking Out Loud About Senior Sex – Joan Price

New Directions in Sex Therapy – Peggy J. Kleinplatz (Editor)

A Place at the Table: The Gay Individual in American Society – Bruce Bawer

Polysecure: Attachment, Trauma, and Consensual Nonmonogamy – Jessica Fern

Sensate Focus in Sex Therapy: The Illustrated Manual – Linda Weiner and Constance Avery-Clark

That's So Gay! Microaggressions and the Lesbian, Gay, Bisexual, and Transgender Community – Kevin Nadal

Trans Sex: Clinical Approaches to Trans Sexualities and Erotic Embodiments – Lucie Fielding

Transforming Sexual Narratives: A Relational Approach to Sex Therapy – Suzanne Iasenza

The Ultimate Guide to Sex and Disability: For All of Us Who Live with Disabilities, Chronic Pain, and Illness – Miriam Kaufman, Cory Silverberg, and Fran Odette

The Velvet Rage: Overcoming the Pain of Growing up Gay in a Straight Man's World – Alan Downs

Sites

The Association of Somatic and Integrative Sexologists (ASIS)

the-asis.org

positivesexuality.org (sex positive research and education)

sexsmartfilms.com (subscription-based videos to share with clients)

sexpositivefamilies.com

surrogatetherapy.org (provides training, consultation, referrals, and professional support)

Glossary

AFAB assigned female at birth. This is typically used to describe someone who has affirmed/transitioned away from the gender they were assigned at birth.

AMAB assigned male at birth. This is typically used to describe someone who has affirmed/transitioned away from the gender they were assigned at birth.

Ableism discrimination and prejudice against persons with disabilities and/or chronic illness.

Aftercare the time (negotiated before play) spent after play to attend to each partner's emotional and physical needs.

Aromantic a broad umbrella identity for anyone who is not romantically attracted to others; however, they may still be comfortable or choose to be in committed platonic relationships that look like traditional romantic relationships to others.

Asexual a broad umbrella identity for anyone who is not sexually attracted to others; however, there is a broad spectrum of asexuality and some who are asexual may still be comfortable or enjoy having sex with others and themselves.

Binary within the LGBTQ+ community, this term often refers to the limiting and incorrect way many people are conditioned to see gender and sexual orientation.

Bisexual someone with the ability to be attracted to both men and women. This does not mean they are 50% into men and 50% into women. It is a spectrum, so, for example, some bisexual people could mostly like men and rarely any women.

Bottoming the act of being subservient and/or receiving during sex.

Cisgender when someone's assigned sex at birth is congruent with their gender.

Cock and ball torture (CBT) sexual play involving pain to or constriction of the penis or testicles.

Compersion in consensually non-monogamous relationships, being happy for a partner when they are enjoying another partner.

Consensual Non-Monogamy (CNM) having multiple sexual and/or romantic partners, in agreement and being honest with their partners. Here are a few types of these relationships, but not all.

- Swinging – when people in a relationship swap partners for sexual experiences.

- Monogamish (term originally coined by Dan Savage) – when partners are usually monogamous, but have certain circumstances when sex is able to occur with others.
- Polyamory (poly) – when partners are able to have a romantic, as well as a sexual, relationship with others.
- Vee – poly relationship where one person is in a romantic relationship with two people and those two people are not in a sexual or romantic relationship with each other.
- Triad (throuple) – poly relationship where all three partners are romantically and/or sexually linked.
- Quad – poly relationship where all four partners are romantically and/or sexually linked.
- Hierarchical Poly – relationship style where one relationship is primary over the other relationships.
- Secondary – a partner outside of the primary relationship.
- Non-hierarchical Poly – relationship where no relationship is deemed more important than any other.
- Relationship Anarchy (RA) – "is both a philosophy and a set of relational practices that seek to minimize the effects of power that are often embedded in hierarchical models" and so "welcomes hybrid relationships that do not fit neatly into usual categories" (Addison & Clason, 2022, p. 304).
- Polyfidelity – when three or more people in a relationship agree to be exclusive, so just in a relationship with each other.
- Solo Non-monogamists – people who lead a single lifestyle and have multiple intimate relationships with others.

Cruising   a somewhat stealthy way of looking at guys around you to see if any would be interested in sex.

Daddy   a dominant partner in a relationship; slang for an older gay man who is involved sexually with a younger man.

Dysphoria   psychological distress caused by an incongruence between one's body presentation and what they know or society deems should be their body presentation.

FTM   female to male. someone who has affirmed their identity as male and was assigned female at birth.

Fluid bonding   having unprotected/barrier-free sex.

Frottage   sex that consists of rubbing the front of one's body against the front of another's body.

Ghosting   after an established contact, no longer communicating with that person without any explanation or warning.

Glory hole   a round cutout in-between bathroom stalls to allow for a penis to be inserted and for people on each side of the stall to engage in, typically, anonymous sex.

Kink   "is simply sexual practices that go beyond what is considered conventional as a means of heightening the intimacy between sexual partners – heightening intimacy being the key component" (Goerlich, 2021, p. 5).

MSM   men who have sex with men. A lot of older research studies would identify test subjects around the behavior of having sex with men, instead of assuming or looking into how the subjects identified in terms of sexual orientation.

MTF   male to female. someone who has affirmed their identity as female and was assigned male at birth.

Masking   not being your authentic self with certain individuals, typically to gain social acceptance or to stay safe from physical or emotional harm.

Metamour   in consensually non-monogamous relationships, the partner of your partner.

Microaggressions   "brief and commonplace daily verbal, behavioral, or environmental indignities, whether intentional or unintentional, that communicate hostile, derogatory, or negative slights and insults towards members of oppressed groups" (Nadal, 2013, p. 36).

Non-binary or Gender Queer   someone who does not identify as either male or female, since gender is a spectrum.

Pansexual   someone who has the ability to be attracted to any other human being.

Poppers   usually come in a small jar and are alkyl nitrites that are inhaled one nostril at a time with the effect being a quick high during sex. This drug is not regulated by the FDA and is often marketed as a cleaning supply so that it can legally be sold in the United States. Actual consumption by a person of poppers is not legal in the United States. Mixing poppers with alcohol use or medication to help with erection can be very dangerous.

PreP (pre-exposure prophylaxis)   introduced in 2012 as a pill you can take once daily that, if taken properly, would leave you at very minimal risk of being able to contract HIV.

Rimming   oral sex performed on someone's anus.

Side   a term (coined by Dr. Joe Kort) for gay men not interested in anal sex.

Surrogate partner therapy   the surrogate partner, the client, and the clinician work together to devise a plan that includes the surrogate being active with the client to better understand what is occurring for them physically and emotionally around sex and then work toward creating and enhancing skills that will resolve these issues.

Topping   the act of being dominant and/or penetrating during sex.

Transgender   an umbrella term for some who do not identify as the gender that they were assigned at birth. Someone who is transgender may decide to change their presentation, body, and/or voice to be more congruent with their identity or may choose not to make any changes and still identity as transgender.

Undetectable viral load   for those who are HIV+, having an HIV viral load so low that it cannot be measured and is extremely unlikely to be passed onto another during sex.

Versatile (Verse)   a term to indicate that someone enjoys both bottoming and topping during sex.

Vulva   genitalia that includes the vaginal canal, labia, and clitoris.

References

Addison, S.M., & Clason, N. (2022). "I will always come home to you:" Affirmative therapy with clients practicing consensual non-monogamy. In R. Harvey, M.J. Murphy, J.J. Bigner, & J.L. Wetchler (Eds.), *Handbook of LGBTQ-affirmative couple and family therapy*. New York, NY: Routledge.

Goerlich, S. (2021). *The leather couch: Clinical practice with kinky clients*. New York, NY: Routledge.

Nadal, K. (2013). *That's so gay! Microaggressions and the lesbian, gay, bisexual, and transgender community*. Washington, DC: American Psychological Association.

Index

For Product Safety Concerns and Information please contact our EU
representative GPSR@taylorandfrancis.com
Taylor & Francis Verlag GmbH, Kaufingerstraße 24, 80331 München, Germany